T0209420

MACAT

An Analysis of

John Maynard Keynes's

The General Theory of Employment, Interest and Money

Dr John Collins

ROUTLEDGE

Published by Macat International Ltd
24:13 Coda Centre, 189 Munster Road, London SW6 6AW.

Distributed exclusively by Routledge
2 Park Square, Milton Park, Abingdon, Oxon OX14 4RN
711 Third Avenue, New York, NY 10017, USA

Routledge is an imprint of the Taylor & Francis Group, an informa business

www.macat.com
info@macat.com

Cataloguing in Publication Data
A catalogue record for this book is available from the British Library.
Library of Congress Cataloguing-in-Publication Data is available upon request.
Cover illustration: Etienne Gilfillan

ISBN 978-1-912302-25-3 (hardback)
ISBN 978-1-912127-90-0 (paperback)
ISBN 978-1-912281-13-8 (e-book)

Notice
The information in this book is designed to orientate readers of the work under analysis,
to elucidate and contextualise its key ideas and themes, and to aid in the development
of critical thinking skills. It is not meant to be used, nor should it be used, as a
substitute for original thinking or in place of original writing or research. References and
notes are provided for informational purposes and their presence does not constitute
endorsement of the information or opinions therein. This book is presented solely for
educational purposes. It is sold on the understanding that the publisher is not engaged
to provide any scholarly advice. The publisher has made every effort to ensure that
this book is accurate and up-to-date, but makes no warranties or representations with
regard to the completeness or reliability of the information it contains. The information
and the opinions provided herein are not guaranteed or warranted to produce particular
results and may not be suitable for students of every ability. The publisher shall not be
liable for any loss, damage or disruption arising from any errors or omissions, or from
the use of this book, including, but not limited to, special, incidental, consequential or
other damages caused, or alleged to have been caused, directly or indirectly, by the
information contained within.

CONTENTS

THE MACAT LIBRARY

The Macat Library is a series of unique academic explorations of seminal works in the humanities and social sciences – books and papers that have had a significant and widely recognised impact on their disciplines. It has been created to serve as much more than just a summary of what lies between the covers of a great book. It illuminates and explores the influences on, ideas of, and impact of that book. Our goal is to offer a learning resource that encourages critical thinking and fosters a better, deeper understanding of important ideas.

Each publication is divided into three Sections: Influences, Ideas, and Impact. Each Section has four Modules. These explore every important facet of the work, and the responses to it.

This Section-Module structure makes a Macat Library book easy to use, but it has another important feature. Because each Macat book is written to the same format, it is possible (and encouraged!) to cross-reference multiple Macat books along the same lines of inquiry or research. This allows the reader to open up interesting interdisciplinary pathways.

To further aid your reading, lists of glossary terms and people mentioned are included at the end of this book (these are indicated by an asterisk [*] throughout) – as well as a list of works cited.

Macat has worked with the University of Cambridge to identify the elements of critical thinking and understand the ways in which six different skills combine to enable effective thinking.
Three allow us to fully understand a problem; three more give us the tools to solve it. Together, these six skills make up the **PACIER** model of critical thinking. They are:

ANALYSIS – understanding how an argument is built
EVALUATION – exploring the strengths and weaknesses of an argument
INTERPRETATION – understanding issues of meaning

CREATIVE THINKING – coming up with new ideas and fresh connections
PROBLEM-SOLVING – producing strong solutions
REASONING – creating strong arguments

To find out more, visit **WWW.MACAT.COM.**

CRITICAL THINKING AND *THE GENERAL THEORY OF EMPLOYMENT, INTEREST AND MONEY*

Primary critical thinking skill: PROBLEM-SOLVING
Secondary critical thinking skill: EVALUATION

John Maynard Keynes's 1936 *General Theory of Employment, Interest and Money* is a perfect example of the global power of critical thinking. A radical reconsideration of some of the founding principles and accepted axioms of classical economics at the time, it provoked a revolution in economic thought and government economic policies across the world.

Unsurprisingly, Keynes's closely argued refutation of the then accepted grounds of economics employs all the key critical thinking skills: analysing and evaluating the old theories and their weaknesses; interpreting and clarifying his own fundamental terms and ideas; problem solving; and using creative thinking to go beyond the old economic theories. Perhaps above all, however, *The General Theory* is a masterclass in problem-solving. Good problem-solvers identify their problem, offer a methodology for resolving it, and suggest solutions.

For Keynes, the problem was both real and theoretical: unemployment. A major issue for governments during the Great Depression, unemployment was also a problem for classical economics. In classical economics, theoretically, unemployment would always disappear. Keynes offered both an explanation of why this was not the case in practice, and a range of solutions that could be implemented through government monetary policy.

ABOUT THE AUTHOR OF THE ORIGINAL WORK

John Maynard Keynes was born in Cambridge in 1883 and read mathematics at King's College, Cambridge. He entered the Civil Service in 1906, but made his name as a thinker when he published a book that fiercely criticized the Versailles Peace Treaty, which ended World War I. However, it was *The General Theory of Employment, Interest and Money*—a meditation on and response to the Great Depression of the early 1930s— that truly cemented Keynes's reputation as one of the most influential economists and intellectuals of the twentieth century. Besides working at the British Treasury, Keynes was also a prolific academic, financial investor, and sponsor of the arts. He died in 1946, aged 62.

ABOUT THE AUTHOR OF THE ANALYSIS

Dr John Collins is a member of the faculty at the London School of Economics, where he is currently Executive Director of the LSE IDEAS International Drug Policy Project.

ABOUT MACAT

GREAT WORKS FOR CRITICAL THINKING

Macat is focused on making the ideas of the world's great thinkers accessible and comprehensible to everybody, everywhere, in ways that promote the development of enhanced critical thinking skills.

It works with leading academics from the world's top universities to produce new analyses that focus on the ideas and the impact of the most influential works ever written across a wide variety of academic disciplines. Each of the works that sit at the heart of its growing library is an enduring example of great thinking. But by setting them in context – and looking at the influences that shaped their authors, as well as the responses they provoked – Macat encourages readers to look at these classics and game-changers with fresh eyes. Readers learn to think, engage and challenge their ideas, rather than simply accepting them.

WAYS IN TO THE TEXT

KEY POINTS

- John Maynard Keynes was an English economist. He was born in 1883 and studied at Eton College and then Cambridge University. He became one of the most important economists of the twentieth century.

- His book *The General Theory of Employment, Interest and Money* outlined a new way of thinking about the economy. Instead of seeing the market as naturally self-correcting (that is, operating without the need for government intervention), *The General Theory* argues that it is prone to prolonged downturns and crises.

- *The General Theory* is the founding text for Keynesian* economics, one of the most influential schools of economic thought of the twentieth century and beyond.

Who Was John Maynard Keynes?

John Maynard Keynes, the author of *The General Theory of Employment, Interest and Money* (1936), was born in Cambridge, United Kingdom, in 1883. He studied at Eton College and King's College, Cambridge, where he read for a degree in mathematics, later attending lectures on economics. In 1906 he entered the Civil Service, the British government's system of administration, working in the India Office. His early career was a blend of academic and civil service work in which he used his understanding of economics to address contemporary government problems. He returned to Cambridge as a lecturer in 1908 and became a Fellow of King's College a year later. He remained at King's until his death in 1946.

After a distinguished period at the British Treasury (the department administering the financial policy of the elected government of the day) during World War I,* he was chosen as the Treasury's financial representative to the Paris Peace Conference* in 1919; this was where the war's victorious nations decided the terms that would be imposed on the defeated nations.[1] After the conference he produced a fierce critique of the peace settlement in a book called *The Economic Consequences of the Peace,* a book declared by Keynes's biographer Robert Skidelsky* to be "one of the most influential books of the twentieth century."[2] The episode earned Keynes a reputation as a leading thinker of his era.

Keynes was unquestionably one of the most influential economists and intellectuals of the twentieth century. In the face of the social and economic crisis of the Great Depression* in the early 1930s, a worldwide economic downturn that began with a stock market crash in the United States, Keynes tried to redefine academic understanding of the economic system. His book *The General Theory of Employment, Interest and Money* fundamentally reshaped the study and implementation of economic thought and policy. In it, he argues that economies are not naturally self-correcting, but instead require government intervention.

What Does *The General Theory* Say?

The General Theory argues that market economies* (roughly, economies in which decisions about investment and distribution, and so on, are driven by the supply* of and demand* for goods) are not self-correcting; likewise, it is not guaranteed that full employment* will return after a temporary economic shock. Keynes says that traditional economics has misunderstood the causes of full employment. According to classical economics,* which holds that the market will naturally find an equilibrium, employment is determined by the price of labor. Keynes though argues that employment is decided by *aggregate**—that is, total—demand. A shortfall in demand will result in a downward cycle: less demand will fuel less employment and then even less demand, resulting in prolonged underemployment. It is for this reason that economies are not self-correcting, and require government intervention.

The onset of the most severe and prolonged depression on record—the Great Depression—caused many to question the core assumption of classical economics, which is that economies self-correct and tend toward full employment and industrial production. Keynes wanted to explain why this is not the case, and why economies instead have an inherent tendency toward instability and sustained economic downturns. As Keynes wrote to his friend George Bernard Shaw,* co-founder of the London School of Economics and Political Science: "I believe myself to be writing a book on economic theory which will largely revolutionize—not, I suppose, at once but in the course of the next ten years—the way the world thinks about its economic problems."[3] In other words, Keynes intended to revolutionize the fundamental ideas underpinning the study of economics.

Keynes's ideas remain of fundamental importance. His work caused an intellectual earthquake in his field that became known as the "Keynesian revolution." Subsequently, economics divided into two main camps. On the one side were liberals* (people whose political positions were founded on principles of liberty and equality) and socialists* (people who held, roughly, that industry should be in public hands); both favored Keynesian assertions that market economies tend to be inherently unstable and therefore require more proactive government policies. On the other side were those with more conservative—right wing—political perspectives, who rejected Keynes's ideas; believing in the effectiveness of market economies, they pointed to the problems of government intervention.

Keynesianism reached its pinnacle in the 1950s and 1960s, when it represented the mainstream in economic policymaking. President Richard Nixon*—a right-wing Republican—proved this point in 1971, when he said, "I am now a Keynesian."[4] Eventually economists such as Milton Friedman* and Friedrich von Hayek,* both champions of the free market, led a successful counterrevolution against Keynesian policymaking during the 1970s and 1980s. They directly influenced policymaking under Prime Minister Margaret Thatcher* in the United Kingdom and President Ronald Reagan* in the United States. With the onset of the global financial crisis in 2007–8,* however, the role of Keynesian policymaking reemerged as a key debate in the study of economics.

Keynes's ideas remain perhaps the most important contribution to the whole field of economics. In 2011, *Time Magazine* listed *The General Theory* as one of the top 100 non-fiction books in English since 1923.[5] According to Google Scholar the book has been cited over 25,671 times as of 2015.[6] It continues to be highly relevant to debates about the role of government in the economy, how to prevent economic downturns and financial crises, and how to ensure economic and political stability.

Why Does *The General Theory* Matter?

The General Theory is a great starting point for all students of modern economics. It inspired the school of economic thought known as Keynesianism and changed the study of economics and the relationship between the state and society. Today, the field of economics remains divided between those subscribing to the Keynesian tradition and those subscribing to the classical tradition.

The key issue in economics remains the relationship and interaction between markets and government policy, and broader society. The reaction of contemporary students to these issues will depend largely on the assumptions they hold about the market. Do they believe, as classical economists do, that markets are inherently self-correcting and that governments should maintain a minimal role? Or do students believe, as Keynesians do, that markets are fundamentally unstable, and prone to recurring crises that can only be stabilized and corrected via government intervention? *The General Theory* is the foundational text for understanding Keynesian tradition. It is vital to any student seeking to understand economics.

For students of other disciplines, *The General Theory* also raises important questions and explores broader intellectual themes. For example, it addresses basic social-psychological and philosophical questions about whether people are indeed "rational," as classical economics assumes. It engages with political and sociological questions about the structure of society, the relationship between the state and the economy, and the broader relationship between citizens and society.

The key questions addressed in Keynes's work are highly relevant to current social questions and policy debates. For example, the financial crisis that began in 2007 raised questions about whether free markets produce the best social outcomes, or are liable to crises and collapse, requiring government oversight and frequent intervention. At a global level, policymakers remain divided over economic policy. Some, particularly in Europe, wish to pursue greater social safety nets and tighter economic regulation. Others, most notably in the US, prefer to unleash the power of the market and the human entrepreneurial spirit. These debates remain unresolved but any student, academic, or politician wishing to engage with them must do so from a basic understanding of Keynesian economics.

NOTES

1 Robert Skidelsky, *John Maynard Keynes: Hopes Betrayed, 1883–1920* (London: Macmillan, 1983).

2 Skidelsky, *John Maynard Keynes,* 384.

3 Johnson Cassidy, "The Demand Doctor," *The New Yorker*, October 10, 2011, accessed September 9, 2015, http://www.newyorker.com/magazine/2011/10/10/the-demand-doctor.

4 Richard Nixon, quoted in Paul Krugman, "Plutocracy, Paralysis, Perplexity," *The New York Times*, May 3, 2012, accessed September 9, 2015, http://www.nytimes.com/2012/05/04/opinion/krugman-plutocracy-paralysis-perplexity.html?_r=0

5 *Time*, "All-Time 100 Nonfiction Books," August 30, 2011. Accessed September 11, 2015. http://entertainment.time.com/2011/08/30/all-time-100-best-nonfiction-books/.

6 Google Scholar, "John Maynard Keynes, *The General Theory of Employment, Interest and Money*," accessed September 24, 2015, https://scholar.google.com/citations?view_op=view_citation&hl=de&user=viLe5BEAAAAJ&citation_for_view=viLe5BEAAAAJ:bFI3QPDXJZMC.

SECTION 1
INFLUENCES

MODULE 1
THE AUTHOR AND THE HISTORICAL CONTEXT

KEY POINTS

- John Maynard Keynes was an English economist. He was born in 1883 and studied at Eton College and then Cambridge University. He became one of the most important economists of the twentieth century.

- His book *The General Theory of Employment, Interest and Money* outlined a new way of thinking about the economy. Instead of seeing the market as naturally self-correcting (that is, operating without the need for government intervention), *The General Theory* argues that it is prone to prolonged downturns and crises.

- *The General Theory* is the founding text for Keynesian* economics, one of the most influential schools of economic thought of the twentieth century and beyond.

Why Read This Text?

John Maynard Keynes's *The General Theory of Employment, Interest and Money* (1936) is the first academic text to systematically detail a role for governments in managing economic downturns and crises. It marked a turning point in the field of economics—away from a strong belief in the efficiency of free markets, toward a greater belief in proactive government policies, demand management* (where the government determines the consumption patterns of individuals and the economy as a whole) and even central economic planning. It is one of the most important economics books of the twentieth century and one of the most important economic texts ever written.

> ❝ This book is chiefly addressed to my fellow economists. I hope that it will be intelligible to others. But its main purpose is to deal with difficult questions of theory, and only in the second place with the applications of this theory to practice. For if orthodox economics is at fault, the error is to be found not in the superstructure, which has been erected with great care for logical consistency, but in a lack of clearness and of generality in the premisses. ❞
>
> John Maynard Keynes, *The General Theory of Employment, Interest and Money*

The Great Depression of the early 1930s saw rates of unemployment reach unprecedented levels in Britain and other industrialized economies. With no single orthodox theory able to explain it or propose policies for recovery, Keynes dedicated himself to writing an alternative theory that would explain the functioning of the economic system. Prior to its publication in 1936, many drafts of *The General Theory* had circulated around Cambridge University.

Economists, historians, and other social scientists continue to debate the policy and academic implications of Keynes's work; virtually all contemporary economic policymaking is in some way determined by an understanding of it. Following the financial crisis that began in 2007,* for example, when Keynesian stimulus policies seemed once again in fashion, one commentator likened the return to Keynesian principles as the return of a master.[1] The key lesson is that Keynes and his writings remain highly relevant to economic and political questions today and also into the foreseeable future.

Author's Life

John Maynard Keynes was born in 1883 in Cambridge, England. His father, John Neville Keynes,* was an economist and senior administrator of the University of Cambridge. His mother, Florence Ada Keynes,* was a social reformer, one of the first women students at the University and the first woman mayor of Cambridge. Keynes studied at Eton College and King's College, Cambridge, where he read for a degree in mathematics and attended lectures on economics. In 1906 he joined the administrative offices of the British government, the Civil Service, at the India Office. He returned to Cambridge as a lecturer in 1908 and became a Fellow of King's College a year later. He remained a Fellow until his death in 1946.

Keynes was one of the most influential economists of the twentieth century. A prolific academic, he was also a financial investor, a sponsor of the arts, and a public servant. He was appointed to the British Treasury—the administrative department charged with implementing economic policy—several times; he participated in negotiations both after World War I* at the Paris Peace Conference*—the meeting at which the victorious nations decided the consequences of defeat for the losing nations in the Treaty of Versailles*—and after World War II* at the Bretton Woods Conference,* when a system of international monetary regulations was established.

Keynes was no stranger to academic or political controversy. His commentary on the Treaty of Versailles—*The Economic Consequences of the Peace* (1920)—was a fierce critique of the policies and leadership of the winning nations, including Britain. He warned that the Carthaginian peace*—that is, the brutal and crushing terms— imposed on Germany would destroy the European economy and undermine political liberalism* (a political position centered on notions of liberty).[2] Keynes's book became an ingrained part of academic orthodoxy in Britain and the United States in the 1920s and is widely viewed as one of the most important factors in the discrediting of the Versailles agreement.[3] The book sold 100,000 copies and was translated into 12 languages.

The General Theory defended the existing capitalist* order (the economic and social system that continues to be shared by Western nations today, in one form or another) in the face of communist* critiques (critiques from those who believe, very roughly, that the path to an equal society is through the abolition of social class and private property, via the total rejection of the capitalist economic and social model). It does this by suggesting a more restrained version of market capitalism, thereby seeking to save capitalism through reform. Keynes's book was widely regarded as a work of genius that transcended the economic crisis of the era. It was clearly not merely a political text, as it also made a unique contribution to the discipline of economics.[4]

Author's Background

The General Theory was published in 1936 amid the Great Depression, the most severe economic downturn of the twentieth century. The crisis began with a stock market crash known as the Wall Street Crash* in September 1929, and was aggravated by the breakdown of the American and international banking systems soon afterward. It caused drastic reductions in output (production), employment, and political stability during the 1930s. International trade declined by 50 percent; in the United States, unemployment peaked at 25 percent, reaching as high as 33 percent in other, harder hit, countries.[5] Around the world the economic crisis had a hugely damaging impact on international security, and contributed to the breakdown of the "collective security" arrangement under the League of Nations* (an international body that served a similar function to the United Nations today). It further undermined the belief in democratic governance and saw the rise of extremely right-wing fascist* governments in a number of countries, particularly Germany, Italy, and Japan.

Keynes therefore wrote and published his book in a context of enormous economic and political upheaval. His goal was both to answer the key economic and political questions of the day and to fundamentally reshape the discipline of economics, and the relationship between governments and the global economy. The dominant classical economists,* who believed that markets should be self-regulating, were unable to explain the intractability and severity of the economic downturn or to propose recovery measures, so a gap emerged between economic theory and reality that demanded a new approach to economics.

NOTES

1   Robert Skidelsky, *Keynes: The Return of the Master* (New York: Public Affairs, 2009).

2   John Maynard Keynes, *The Economic Consequences of the Peace* (New York: Harcourt Brace, 1920).

3   Etienne Mantoux, *The Carthaginian Peace: Or the Economic Consequences of Mr Keynes*, (Oxford: Oxford University Press, 1946).

4   Axel Leijonhufvud, *On Keynesian Economics and the Economics of Keynes* (London: Oxford University Press, 1968), 35.

5   Ben Bernanke and Robert H Frank, Principles Of Microeconomics (Boston: McGraw-Hill/Irwin, 2007).

ACADEMIC CONTEXT

KEY POINTS

- Economics can be defined as "the study of market outcomes and resource allocation within a society and their interaction with the state."

- Economics is largely divided along classical* and modern liberal* lines. Classical economists argue that markets are efficient and produce the best outcomes, and that they should therefore operate free of government interference. Modern liberals argue that markets are inefficient, liable to crises, and produce inequality—and therefore require strong and frequent government interference.

- *The General Theory* is often viewed as the founding academic text in the main liberal school of economic thought: Keynesianism.*

The Work in its Context

John Maynard Keynes's *The General Theory of Employment, Interest and Money* was written as an economics text. As Keynes wrote in the preface: "This book is chiefly addressed to my fellow economists. I hope that it will be intelligible to others. But its main purpose is to deal with difficult questions of theory, and only in the second place with the applications of this theory to practice."[1] However, it also touches on core issues relating to politics, philosophy, social psychology, history, and policy formation.

Economics is the branch of social sciences that studies the interaction between the production, distribution, and consumption of goods and services. Before the nineteenth century it was referred to as

> 66 He was in the direct line of great British economists from Adam Smith to John Stuart Mill, making it his first business to study the facts and to see to it that his conclusions were consistent with common sense. But although he lay in the tradition he was also a revolutionary. Not since Ricardo has economic theory leapt forward so swiftly as in the years that followed the appearance in the spring of 1930 of the 'Treatise on Money.' 99
>
> *The Economist*, "John Maynard Keynes"

"political economy" to highlight its interaction with social and political theories. Following the publication of *An Inquiry into the Nature and Causes of the Wealth of Nations* (1776) by the influential Scottish economist Adam Smith,* the field gradually became known as "economics." It also became more concerned with a systematic analysis of economic forces and activity, in order to understand how economies work and what role government and social policy have in regulating and facilitating them.

Economics as a discipline has developed several schools and sub-schools. The most important are classical economics; neoclassical economics* (an approach to economics founded on the principles that people are rational and have discernible preferences based on value; that people maximize utility while firms maximize profits; and that people act independently with full and relevant information); Keynesian economics; monetarism* (the theory that the government can stabilize the economy by controlling the amount of money in circulation); and Marxist economics* (an approach to economics founded on the analyses of the German economist and social philosopher Karl Marx).*

Within these schools are a large number of sub-branches, with approaches that differ ideologically, epistemologically,* (in their philosophical analysis of knowledge) or methodologically (in their method of research and analysis).

Keynesian economics began with the publication of *The General Theory*. The book introduced a new theoretical and policy framework based on principles of strong government intervention in the economy. It challenged classical assumptions that had been the key philosophical foundation for the discipline since the publication of Adam Smith's *Wealth of Nations* in 1776.

Overview of the Field

While the discipline of economics dates back to early human civilizations, the theoretical study on which modern economics is founded can be traced to the publication of Adam Smith's *Wealth of Nations*. Smith developed many of the ideas and concepts still used in the study of economics today, such as the "division of labor" (in which individuals cooperate to undertake specific specialized tasks, thus increasing productivity) and the "gains from trade" (in which voluntary trading increases the wealth of both participants). Smith's ideas are generally seen as the earliest example of the classical school of economics. They were later developed by early economics scholars from Britain, David Ricardo* and John Stuart Mill.*

Later schools of thought elaborated on the ideas of Smith and the role of the economy in political life. Karl Marx (1818–83), for example, focused on the "labor theory of value" and essentially sought to explain how labor is exploited by capital (a word used as shorthand, roughly, for the social and economic system of capitalism*—and those who benefit from it at the expense of those who do the labor).

Classical economics became neoclassical economics toward the end of the nineteenth century, following what has been called the "marginal revolution." This tried to apply principles of marginal utility* (the measurement of the benefit derived from buying an additional unit of some good or service) to the field of economic enquiry, using scientific objectivity rather than social theory as a measure.[2] It is within this context of debate between classical, neoclassical, and Marxist economics that Keynes published *The General Theory*.

Academic Influences

Keynes's *The General Theory* represents a departure from classical theory, the dominant theory of the period. Keynes used the term "classical" to refer not only to the predecessors and founders of Ricardian* economics, believed by Marx to be David Ricardo and James Mill,* but also the followers of the Ricardian theory, including James Mill's son John Stuart Mill, the British economist Alfred Marshall,* the Irish social philosopher Francis Edgeworth,* and the British economist Arthur Pigou.*[3]

Alfred Marshall and Arthur Pigou, fellow economists at the University of Cambridge, were Keynes's main mentors. He was brought up on their ideas, which he taught in his lectures for many years. Keynes said: "The composition of this book has been for the author a long struggle of escape … from habitual modes of thought and expression. … The difficulty lies, not in the new ideas, but in escaping from the old ones, which ramify, for those brought up as most of us have been, into every corner of our minds."[4]

Keynes based his understanding of the classical theory on the work of Arthur Pigou in his *Theory of Unemployment*.[5] Keynes calls this "the only detailed account of the classical theory of employment which exists." Pigou's analysis, Keynes points out, "makes the volume of employment to depend on two fundamental factors, namely (1) the real rates of wages for which workpeople stipulate, and (2) the shape of the Real Demand Function for Labour."[6] Keynes tried to undermine this theory by arguing that employment instead derives from the total demand* in an economy.

Although there were other schools of economic thought at the time, such as Marxism* (an approach to economics founded on the political, social, and economic analysis of Karl Marx), ideas were generally fixed in the classical framework, "upon which I was brought up and which dominates the economic thought, both practical and theoretical, of the governing and academic classes of this generation, as it has for a hundred years past."[7] *The General Theory* argues against the dominant ideology, which was unable to provide either an explanation for or solution to the problems in the economy.

NOTES

1   John Maynard Keynes, preface to *The General Theory of Employment, Interest and Money, The Collected Writings of John Maynard Keynes, Vol 7* (London: Macmillan St. Martin's Press, 1973), XXI.

2   Roberto Mangabeira Unger, *Free Trade Reimagined: The World Division of Labor and the Method of Economics* (Princeton: Princeton University Press, 2007), 55–64.

3   Keynes, *The General Theory*, 3.

4   Keynes, *The General Theory*, XXII.

5   A. C. Pigou, *The Theory Of Unemployment* (London: Macmillan, 1933).

6   Keynes, *The General Theory*, 272.

7   Keynes, *The General Theory*, XXI.

MODULE 3
THE PROBLEM

KEY POINTS

- *The General Theory* tries to explain the key economic question of the 1930s, while asking more general questions such as: Why do economies fail? Why does unemployment persist? Can governments intervene to correct it?

- Keynes claims that prolonged unemployment is not caused simply by the refusal of labor to accept lower wages.

- Keynes rejects classical economics* and its assertion that wage corrections inevitably lead to full employment,* without the interference of government policy. He argues that it is aggregate demand*—the total demand for goods and services in an economy at a given time—that determines levels of employment.

Core Question

John Maynard Keynes's book *The General Theory* was published during an era of enormous economic and political upheaval. The economic downturn known as the Great Depression* had produced a collapse in international trade and employment. Democracies and market economies, such as those of Germany, Japan, and Italy, were failing as populations looked to totalitarian and autocratic regimes (that is, governments run by dictators who deprived their people of liberty) to ensure economic growth and employment. Meanwhile classical economic theory struggled to explain the continued high unemployment. A collapse in the wage rate, according to traditional theory, should have caused a fall in unemployment. Keynes tries to engage with these key issues, examining why free market economies

66 The contention that the unemployment which characterizes a depression is due to a refusal by labour to accept a reduction of money-wages is not clearly supported by the facts. **99**

John Maynard Keynes, *The General Theory of Employment, Interest and Money*

might fail to produce full employment and how governments could intervene to correct this, while still maintaining the core structure of a market economy.

In a broader sense Keynes addressed a key question of economics: what are the causes or determinants of economic output, growth, and employment? Classical economics argued that the price of labor was the sole determinant of employment and that competitive markets would, in the long run, result in full employment. The length and severity of the Great Depression, however, appeared to disprove this claim; in the United States, unemployment reached 25 percent. Keynes suggested that "aggregate demand" (the expenditure of money within the economy) was the determinant that economists were looking for.

The Participants

Although many questioned the failures of the market economy during the Great Depression, the debate took place within traditional explanatory frameworks. Marxists* highlighted the Great Depression as an example of the inherent instability of the market economy, and a reason for an economic and political revolution.

Free market, or classical, economists suggested that wage deflation—a decrease in workers' wages—could bring about a return to full employment. Policymakers who followed classical economics' solutions, such as Herbert Hoover,* US president during the Great

Depression, pushed for balanced budget and liquidation policies.* These were policies that would "purge" excesses from the economy[1] by allowing the collapse of investments, which in turn would bring about a new, more stable, economic equilibrium. US Treasury Secretary Andrew W. Mellon* advised President Hoover that if they wished to combat the depression they must "liquidate labor, liquidate stocks, liquidate farmers, liquidate real estate ... it will purge the rottenness out of the system. High costs of living and high living will come down. People will work harder, live a more moral life. Values will be adjusted, and enterprising people will pick up from less competent people." Although Hoover rejected many of Mellon's proposals, they highlighted an important strand of thinking at the time.[2]

Keynes offered a different solution. He rejected the Marxist approach, which viewed the Great Depression as vindication for the worldview that capitalism* is inherently unstable. Instead, Keynes offered a justification for the continuation of capitalism. As the Nobel Prize-winning economist Paul Krugman* writes: "Keynes was no socialist—he came to save capitalism, not to bury it."[3] Keynes suggested a new explanation for the market failures, and a way for governments to lessen them. This contradicted the liquidationist approach of Mellon and classical economists.

The Contemporary Debate

Keynes approaches the question by dealing first with the classical theory and its assumptions. He is especially critical of the theory that "supply* creates its own demand." According to this theory, long-term "involuntary unemployment" is impossible because, as the price of labor falls, an excess supply creates demand for it. Thus, classical economists claimed, economies would always tend towards full employment. Keynes addresses his intended target clearly, writing: "Those, who are strongly wedded to what I shall call 'the classical theory,' will fluctuate, I expect, between a belief that I am quite wrong and a belief that I am saying nothing new." Further he expects his tone and "sharp distinctions" will produce "controversy." Nevertheless, he tries to "attack" theories that "I myself held with conviction for many years."[4] Keynes attempts to undermine a school of economic thought to which he had previously subscribed. Further, he does it in a way that he knows will cause controversy and even flat rejection from other economists.

Keynes's book is the beginning of a new paradigm—that is, an altogether new conceptual model—for understanding the functioning of the economy. To fully appreciate his contribution, it is important to understand the evolution of the discipline of economics since the publication of Adam Smith's* *An Inquiry into the Nature and Causes of the Wealth of Nations* of 1776.

Keynes claims that he wrote the book for his "fellow economists." He expects his readers to understand the principles of classical and neoclassical* economics and their central proposition that free markets will tend toward full employment.[5]

NOTES

1   J. Bradford De Long, "'Liquidation' Cycles: Old Fashioned Real Business Cycle Theory and the Great Depression," National Bureau of Economic Research, Working Paper 3546 (1990): 5.

2   Herbert Hoover, *The Memoirs of Herbert Hoover, Volume 3: The Great Depression* (New York: The Macmillan Company, 1952), accessed September 9, 2015, http://www.ecommcode.com/hoover/ebooks/pdf/FULL/B1V3_Full.pdf.

3   Paul R. Krugman, introduction to *The General Theory Of Employment, Interest And Money* by John Maynard Keynes (Basingstoke, Hampshire; New York: Palgrave Macmillan, 2007).

4   John Maynard Keynes, *The General Theory of Employment, Interest and Money, The Collected Writings of John Maynard Keynes, Vol 7* (London: Macmillan/St. Martin's Press, 1973), xxi.

5   Keynes, *The General Theory*, xxi.

THE AUTHOR'S CONTRIBUTION

KEY POINTS

- Keynes argues that unemployment is determined by aggregate demand* (the sum total of all demand* for goods and services in the economy), not the price of labor.

- The idea that unemployment is caused by shortfalls in aggregate demand revolutionized the way economists viewed the role of government and policy in altering economic outcomes.

- Keynes engages with existing economic theory, but tries to revolutionize it through new ideas and frameworks.

Author's Aims

John Maynard Keynes's book *The General Theory* aimed to "revolutionize ... the way the world thinks about its economic problems."[1] Keynes wanted to provide an alternative theoretical framework for understanding the field of economics. Whereas classical economists* had argued that employment was determined by the price of labor, Keynes argued that employment was determined by what he called "aggregate demand" within an economy. As one commentator writes, *The General Theory* "is first and foremost a theory of employment ... A theory of employment is then a theory of the decisions of employers to hire labor and of employees to offer their services."[2]

Keynes's argument contradicts the theoretical underpinning of classical economics, which holds that, as one commentator writes, "if prices are perfectly flexible, involuntary unemployment can arise only

> ❝ The ideas of economists and political philosophers, both when they are right and when they are wrong, are more powerful than is commonly understood. Indeed the world is ruled by little else. Practical men, who believe themselves to be quite exempt from any intellectual influence, are usually the slaves of some defunct economist. ❞
>
> John Maynard Keynes, *The General Theory of Employment, Interest and Money*

from frictional delays in the physical changeover from serving one market to another … therefore all 'non-employment' is either voluntary or frictional."[3]

This implies that involuntary unemployment of a sustained nature, the kind witnessed during the Great Depression,* is not only possible, it is a likely outcome of a free market economy. Further, government intervention to correct this outcome is not only possible but also desirable.

Approach

Keynes built *The General Theory* on lectures and earlier works published after 1932. In 1933, publications such as the papers "A Monetary Theory of Production," "The Means to Prosperity," "The Multiplier," "The Distinction Between a Co-operative Economy and an Entrepreneur Economy," and a biographical sketch of Thomas Malthus*[4] showed the direction Keynes's ideas were taking. All these publications reflected his dissatisfaction with the dominant belief in free markets and minimal government intervention.

Keynes distinguishes between a real exchange economy* (an economy based on the exchange and barter of real commodities rather than mechanisms for transaction, such as money) and a monetary economy. In a real exchange economy, money is neutral and simply acts as means of exchange. This basic assumption supports the classical quantity theory of money* (the theory that prices are affected by the amount of money in circulation).

In a monetary economy, however, money works as a store of wealth as well. Money, Keynes wrote, "plays a part of its own and affects motives and decisions and is, in short, one of the operative factors in the situation, so that the course of events cannot be predicted, either in the long period or in the short, without a knowledge of the behavior of money between the first state and the last."[5] This type of capitalist* economy (the dominant model today in the United States, Europe, and increasingly throughout Asia and Africa), subject to booms and depressions, is the one he considers as he formulates the argument made throughout *The General Theory*. The way Keynes combines his ideas and themes marks a departure from the classical theory—according to which market forces lead the economy to equilibrium through the price mechanism (which efficiently allocates all available resources)—and from Say's Law,* a theory named after the French economist Jean Baptiste Say* according to which "supply* creates its own demand."[6] More importantly, it rejects the orthodox notion that the economy naturally tends toward an equilibrium in which full employment* occurs.

Contribution in Context

Keynes incorporates and develops many existing economic concepts in his text. He uses them to justify his overarching argument that contemporary understandings of the economy were incorrect. According to classical economics, as we have just seen, economies tend toward equilibrium and full employment in the long run, a view stemming from Say's Law.

Say's Law says that supply creates its own demand, and that therefore a "general glut"*—meaning an overabundant supply—of excess goods or labor cannot exist. Or as Keynes writes, "the whole of the costs of production must necessarily be spent in the aggregate, directly or indirectly, on purchasing the product."[7] Keynes points to the Great Depression as an empirical example (that is, an example verifiable by observable evidence) that general gluts can exist. Further he tries to develop a new theoretical framework that undermines Say's Law.

Keynes restates Say's Law in a different way, writing that "supply creates its own demand in the sense that the aggregate demand price is equal to the aggregate supply price for all levels of output and employment."[8] He argues that investment and supply are not independent of one another and, therefore, will not tend toward balance. He goes on to argue that financial markets are governed by speculative behavior. In this equation, speculation is determined both by investors' personal perceptions of the market and by their perception of other investors' perceptions. This results in markets being ruled not by rational investment choices but by "animal spirits."[9] In this situation, stability is not the inevitable outcome of markets; instead, markets tend toward a variety of equilibriums that can under-employ people and resources.

NOTES

1   Johnson Cassidy, "The Demand Doctor," *The New Yorker*, October 10, 2011.

2   Mark Hayes, preface to *The Economics Of Keynes* (Cheltenham, UK: Edward Elgar, 2006).

3   Hayes, *The Economics Of Keynes*, 46.

4   John Maynard Keynes, *The General Theory of Employment, Interest and Money, The Collected Writings of John Maynard Keynes, Vol 7* (London: Macmillan/St. Martin's Press, 1973), xii. These publications are presented in other volumes of the author's *Collected Writings*. "A Monetary Theory of Production" appears in volume 13, "The Means to Prosperity" in volume 9, "The Multiplier" is included in an edition of "The Means to Prosperity," "The Distinction Between a Co-operative Economy and an Entrepreneur Economy" appears in volume 29, and "Thomas Robert Malthus: The First of the Cambridge Economists" in volume 10.

5   Keynes, *The General Theory*, 408–9. For a complementary discussion, see Keynes, "Co-operative Economy and Entrepreneur Economy," 76–87.

6   Robert W. Clower, "5: Trashing J. B. Say: The Story of a Mare's Nest," In K. Vela Velupillai, *Macroeconomic Theory and Economic Policy: Essays in Honour of Jean-Paul Fitoussi*, (London: Routledge, 2004).

7   Keynes, *The General Theory*, 23.

8   Keynes, *The General Theory*, 21–2.

9   Keynes, *The General Theory,* 162.

SECTION 2
IDEAS

MAIN IDEAS

KEY POINTS

- Keynes argues that the level of employment in an economy is determined not by the price of labor, but rather by the level of aggregate demand* (the sum total of the demand for goods in services in any economy).

- Free and competitive markets will not necessarily produce full employment.* Instead, underemployment and low economic output can be a sustained feature of market economies unless governments intervene.

- Keynes presents his ideas by picking apart many of the underpinnings of classical economic* theory and proposing a new way of thinking about how a market economy functions.

Key Themes

John Maynard Keynes's overarching argument in *The General Theory of Employment, Interest and Money* is that the market economy is inherently unstable, and liable to prolonged recessions and depressions. As Keynes writes, it is "primarily a study of the forces which determine changes in the scale of output and employment as a whole."[1]

Previously, "classical" economists believed that the supply* of goods and services is always less than demand* and that, therefore, there will always be demand for goods; once the market has determined the correct price for a good, demand removes excess supplies. This was referred to as Say's Law* (a principle named after the French economist Jean Baptiste Say).* An important supporter of this classical view was the late eighteenth and early nineteenth-century

> **❝** Keynes was no socialist—he came to save capitalism, not to bury it ... Keynes wrote during a time of mass unemployment, of waste and suffering on an incredible scale. A reasonable man might well have concluded that capitalism had failed, and that only huge institutional changes—perhaps the nationalization of the means of production—could restore economic sanity ... Yet Keynes argued that these failures had surprisingly narrow, technical causes. **❞**
>
> Paul Krugman, introduction to *The General Theory of Employment, Interest and Money*, 2007 edition

economist David Ricardo.*

Classical economists developed this argument further to argue that employment is determined by the price of labor. Keynes, however, argues that aggregate demand determines employment. He believes that a shortfall in demand will result in a downward cycle, reducing employment and further demand, so creating long-term underemployment. The implication is that economies are not, as classical economists believed, self-correcting.

The text also implies that there is a role for governments in managing and stabilizing the general economy. By intervening through fiscal policy* (government spending and taxation) and monetary policy* (the deliberate control of the amount of money in circulation in an economy), the government can increase aggregate demand. It can also cool the excessive accumulation of unsold products—something that should be avoided in order to prevent cautious investors and firms from overreacting by curtailing production and laying off workers. The overarching political implication and theme of Keynes's work is that governments have a role in facilitating the efficient use of economic resources. Their interventions in the economy do not merely threaten the efficient workings of a self-regulating market, as classical economists believed.

Exploring the Ideas

Keynes argues that government could solve the Great Depression by increasing the "inducement to invest," either by reducing interest rates (monetary policy) or spending money on infrastructure (fiscal policy).[2]

Classical economists believed that unemployment could be reduced by lowering the wage rate. However, Keynes argued that the classical theory of employment was based on "two fundamental postulates." The first is that "the wage is equal to the marginal product* of labor" or the value of its marginal output.* The "marginal product" is the change in output that results from adding one additional unit of a specific input—so the "marginal output" of fertilizer, for example, is the amount of additional crop it produces. Second, that the real wage* paid is "just sufficient" to persuade the workers to voluntarily offer their labor.

Following these principles, labor market outcomes were viewed as being determined by the supply of, and demand for, labor, and tend toward a balanced situation in which the supply of labor is absorbed by demand. Under these circumstances, unemployment is something abnormal caused by shocks, which eventually clears under free-market conditions in which wages can fall.

This, as Keynes wrote, "is the substance of Professor Pigou's* *Theory of Unemployment*—the only detailed account of the classical theory of employment which exists."[3] The implication is that employers and employees, if they are free to negotiate wages, will eventually reach a position of full employment.

Keynes argues that the classical approach is based on a mistaken belief that bargaining between the supply and demand for labor will alter "real wages."* He warns both that, in fact, laborers might refuse lower wages and that if wages decrease, so do prices. This means that "real wages"—what a laborer can actually can afford to buy with what she or he earns—remain the same. This being the case, unemployment is not reduced, as classical economists claim.[4]

Keynes then argues that unemployment is actually determined by other factors. In particular he looks at "involuntary" unemployment, "the possibility of which the classical theory does not admit." Keynes argues that since involuntary unemployment clearly does exist, economists should reject the incorrect assertions of classical economics.[5]

Overall, Keynes argues that aggregate spending (the total amount people spend in the economy after savings) determines demand and therefore employment. This also explains the existence of involuntary unemployment. If people are not spending, businesses are not selling—and so they are not hiring.[6]

Language and Expression

The General Theory was aimed at an academic and expert audience. Keynes writes, as we have seen, that the book is "chiefly addressed to my fellow economists. I hope that it will be intelligible to others. But its main purpose is to deal with difficult questions of theory, and only in the second place with the applications of this theory to practice." Furthermore, he wrote it to be "controversial."[7] Although the basic premises of Keynesian* economics will be familiar to the general public, it is unlikely that the work is widely read outside the world of economics.

The General Theory is widely considered to be a poorly written text. Some have called it "wrong in many of its most important assertions, as well as being disorganized, confusing, and self-contradicting."[8] In 1946, the notable Keynesian economist Paul Samuelson* went so far as to describe it as "a badly written book, poorly organized; any layman who, beguiled by the author's previous reputation, bought the book was cheated of his five shillings. It is not well suited for classroom use. It is arrogant, bad tempered, polemical and not overly generous in its acknowledgements. It abounds in mares' nests and confusions. In short, it is a work of genius."[9]

The badly written nature of the text has led to differing interpretations and has contributed to the splintering of Keynesianism into different schools of thought.[10] Nevertheless, its rich and often confusing language has inspired much discussion.

NOTES

1 John Maynard Keynes, *The General Theory of Employment, Interest and Money, The Collected Writings of John Maynard Keynes, Vol 7,* (London: Macmillan/St. Martin's Press, 1973), xxi.

2 Keynes, *General Theory,* 27.

3 Keynes, *General Theory*, 7.

4 Keynes, *General Theory*, 7–8.

5 Keynes, General Theory, 21.

6 Keynes, General Theory, 37–46.

7 Keynes, *General Theory,* xxi.

8 Clifford F. Thies, "The Paradox of Thrift: RIP," *Cato Journal*, 16, no. 1 (1996): 122.

9 P. A. Samuelson, "The General Theory," *Econometrica* 14 (July), Reprinted in H. Lekachman (ed.) *Keynes' General Theory* (New York: St. Martin's Press, [1946] 1964), 316.

10 Thies, "Paradox of Thrift," 122.

MODULE 6
SECONDARY IDEAS

KEY POINTS

- Markets do not necessarily produce the best outcomes. Consumers often increase consumption at a slower rate than the increase in their income. Falling wages do not necessarily result in rising employment. The market for investment and savings is complex and frequently produces outcomes that are not ideal.

- These secondary ideas are an attempt by Keynes to explain many of the inefficiencies and instabilities of the market economy.

- The most important secondary idea in *The General Theory* is that consumption does not increase in proportion to income—an idea explained by the "marginal propensity to consume."*

Other Ideas

The key contribution of John Maynard Keynes's *The General Theory* was to take existing theories and ideas and either flatly reject them, or strongly rethink them. The overarching school of thought he engaged with is known as classical* or neoclassical economics.* Keynes tackles a number of key subject areas within this school. The first—which he calls his "main theme"—is the "marginal propensity to consume." This measures the degree of increased spending that is produced by an increase in income. It shows what percentage of each additional dollar earned is then spent, as opposed to how much is saved and invested.

Keynes also questions the classical view of how wages are determined. Classical economics claims that flexible wages would

> ❖❖ Thus, given the propensity to consume and the rate of new investment, there will be only one level of employment consistent with equilibrium; since any other level will lead to inequality between the aggregate supply* price of output as a whole and its aggregate demand price ... The effective demand associated with full employment is a special case, only realised when the propensity to consume and the inducement to invest stand in a particular relationship to one another. ❖❖
>
> John Maynard Keynes, *The General Theory of Employment, Interest and Money*

result in the supply of labor being absorbed by demand. Keynes argues, however, that during wage negotiations, employers and workers set nominal wages* (that is, wages that do not take into account the fact that the price of goods increases), not real wages* (a wage rate adjusted for the increase in prices). This means that prices are a factor in these negotiations. If wages fall while prices remain the same, the purchasing power of workers is reduced—and overall demand* for goods declines. Classical economics, Keynes argues, is therefore wrong to conclude that a decrease in wages is the solution to recession and unemployment; instead, falling wages make a recession worse by reducing consumer spending power and potentially sparking a downward economic spiral.[1]

Keynes also questions the efficiency of saving and investment decisions. He argues that a fall in consumer demand or a loss of business confidence can result in a fall in investment. This can then produce excessive saving, leading in turn to a misallocation of economic resources and a decline in economic output and employment.

Secondary ideas such as these help form Keynes's central thesis of market inefficiency, and the potential of free markets to produce outcomes that are not ideal.

Exploring the Ideas

Keynes claimed that his "main theme" was to pick apart the classical theory of consumption. Notably, he argues that the marginal propensity to consume* is less than one—in other words: a rise in income does not automatically lead to a similar rise in expenditure and demand (a \$1 rise in income, for example, may only lead to an \$0.80 rise in spending). Explaining this, he writes: "The fundamental psychological law, upon which we are entitled to depend with great confidence both *a priori* from our knowledge of human nature and from the detailed facts of experience, is that men are disposed, as a rule and on the average, to increase their consumption as their income increases, but not by as much as the increase in their income."

His conclusion is that "every weakening in the propensity to consume regarded as a permanent habit must weaken the demand for capital as well as the demand for consumption."[2]

Keynes also examined the allocation of savings and investment. Whereas classical economists maintained that these decisions were best left to the free market, Keynes suggested that they could be subject to major failures. Classical economists had previously argued that interest rates (that is, the return on savings or the cost of borrowing) tend to fall in response to an excess of "loanable funds," discouraging additional savings and encouraging investment. Keynes provides a complicated explanation as to why this classical expectation is incorrect, showing that savings do not fall as quickly as interest rates.[3]

One element of Keynes's examination of savings and investment was his elaboration of the idea of a "liquidity trap."* Traditional economic theory held that injections of money into the banking system increase the supply of money and reduce the rate of interest. Keynes warned, however, that in the liquidity trap scenario, interest rates are not reduced because people expect economic deflation* (that is, falling wages and prices) and decide to hoard cash as insurance. An increase in the supply of money does not, therefore, increase prices by way of inflation.* A better policy intervention for governments is to inject money into the economy by spending on things such as construction projects.[4] This is one of the reasons Keynes is often viewed as favoring fiscal policy* (policies concerning government spending) over monetary policy* (policies controlling the amount of money in circulation) as a means to stimulate economic growth.

Overlooked

The General Theory remains one of the most important and controversial texts in the history of economics. According to Google Scholar, it has been cited over 25,671 times as of 2015.[5] There is little evidence that any aspects of the work remain overlooked. The book has spawned entire generations and schools of economic thought; vigorous debates over its implications and interpretations continue to this day. That said, there is likely to be a continued development of Keynesian* thought as economic circumstances, evidence, and theory evolve. Certain aspects of the book are sure to change in relative significance and previously underemphasized parts are likely to receive new attention.

Some have argued that there has been too much emphasis on those aspects of *The General Theory* that focus on the technical implications of fiscal and monetary policies. Keynes had "concern" for the "conflict between manufacturers (enterprise) and greed (speculation and 'high finance')" and argued that "the main positive proposal of *The General Theory* is not discretionary fiscal policy but the severe curbing of 'high finance.'"[6] In other words, those arguing for a rethink of Keynesian economics suggest that the book tends to focus too much on the role of government in managing supply and demand in the economy, preventing its application to questions of financial speculation and the need to curb the power of financial markets.

The constant reinterpretations and reengagement with Keynes's work, and the extent to which different parties have come to very different conclusions, indicate the text's fundamental strength.

NOTES

1   John Maynard Keynes, *The General Theory of Employment, Interest and Money, The Collected Writings of John Maynard Keynes, Vol 7* (London: Macmillan/St. Martin's Press, 1973), 257–69.

2   Keyes, *The General Theory*, 89–106.

3   Keynes, *The General Theory*, 135–256

4   Keynes, *The General Theory*, 135–256.

5   Google Scholar, "John Maynard Keynes, *The General Theory of Employment, Interest and Money*," accessed September 24, 2015, https://scholar.google.com/citations?view_op=view_citation&hl=de&user =viLe5BEAAAAJ&citation_for_view=viLe5BEAAAAJ:bFI3QPDXJZMC,

6   Piero V. Mini, *John Maynard Keynes* (London: Palgrave Macmillan, 1994), 90–1.

MODULE 7
ACHIEVEMENT

KEY POINTS

- John Maynard Keynes revolutionized the study of economics. He inspired a new era of government policies, known as Keynesian* policies, aimed at economic management.

- Keynes's achievement came as a result of a widespread loss of confidence in classical economics* during the Great Depression* of the 1930s, and the desire for greater state control of the economy following World War II.*

- Perhaps the greatest limitation on the theory was the inability of Keynes to develop its key ideas due to ill health, his preoccupation with postwar planning, and his death in 1946.

Assessing the Argument

John Maynard Keynes's book *The General Theory of Employment, Interest and Money* fundamentally reshaped the study and practice of economics and government policy. When Keynes wrote the book he intended to "revolutionize" economic theory and "the way the world thinks about its economic problems."[1] To this end he was entirely successful. Keynes's obituary in the *Economist* in 1946 noted that he had already transformed economic thought with his earlier publications; although "the *General Theory* of 1936 is the Keynesian bible," it read, his earlier work "the *Treatise [on Money]* nonetheless, is by far the greater book in the history of economic thought. Orthodox economics, up to then, had been obsessed with the analysis of static conditions, the detailed examination of one snapshot of a rapidly moving process. Keynes, in the *Treatise*, made the transition from statics

> **❝** Never again will it be possible for the state to regard the course of prices, the level of the national income or the volume of employment as things outside its control. **❞**
>
> *Economist,* "John Maynard Keynes"

to dynamics; he converted economics into a study of the flow of incomes and expenditures and, in so doing, opened up whole new vistas before the economist."[2]

By the 1960s, the ideas outlined in *The General Theory* had conquered the field of economic thought. In 1966, Milton Friedman,* perhaps the leading anti-Keynesian economist of the twentieth century, wrote: "In one sense, we are all Keynesians now."[3] It was a sentiment echoed in 1971 by Republican US President Richard Nixon[x] who, upon removing the US from the gold standard* (a monetary system in which the standard economic unit is related to the price of gold) was quoted as saying, "I am now a Keynesian in economic policy."[4]

It is for such reasons that Keynes is regarded as one of the most important economic thinkers of all time, and *The General Theory* is universally considered his greatest work. The policy implications of Keynes's work and its theoretical underpinnings remain highly contested and debated, even among those who subscribe to Keynesian economics. There is no doubt that Keynes achieved his goal of changing the way the world thought about economic questions and government policy.

Achievement in Context

Keynes's core ideas changed the way economists analyzed unemployment and recessions. Keynes wanted to revise classical economic theory, which did not allow for the idea of "involuntary" unemployment, and had therefore rejected a role for government in managing aggregate demand* in the economy.

The theory of classical economics rests on two propositions. The first is, very roughly, that wages tend to equal the productivity of labor. The second is that wages tend to equal the marginal disutility* of labor to the laborer (in other words, a laborer will only supply an additional hour of labor if the gain in wages equals the loss of leisure time). When the loss of leisure time outvalues the additional gain in wages, the laborer will cease to labor. Classical economics holds that where markets can adjust, the only unemployment that can be sustained is that held by people between jobs and by those voluntarily unemployed.

The global response to the 2007–8 financial crisis* and the subsequent economic downturn highlighted the extent to which Keynesian economics had become established in governments' views on managing economic crises. Governments around the world coordinated massive economic stimulus to prevent a deflationary spiral* (an economic phenomenon in which falling prices cause decreases in wages, which in turn causes prices to be adjusted downward—and so on), to stimulate demand,* and to increase employment. They did this through both monetary* and fiscal* policies (that is, through policies concerning the management of the amount of money in the economy and through government spending).

Regarding monetary policy, central banks around the world purchased $2.5 trillion worth of debt from governments and assets from banks. This was the largest expansion of the money supply,* or liquidity injection, in world history. Further, the US governments and governments across Europe directly intervened to increase the capital holding of their banks by $1.5 trillion.[5] The subsequent stabilization of the banking system and the avoidance of a second Great Depression* was hailed as an example of government success. US President Barack

Obama* declared in 2010 "the markets are now stabilized, and we've recovered most of the money we spent on the banks."[6]

Regarding fiscal policy, governments around the world undertook a massive expansion of government borrowing and spending, in line with Keynesian theory. Some, such as the UK, later reversed these fiscal expansions and embarked on a policy of "austerity"* (in which spending cuts and tax increases are implemented in order to manage deficits). The largest of these fiscal expansions was in the US, where the American Recovery and Reinvestment Act of 2009 represented a $787 billion stimulus package aimed at increasing demand and employment through tax cuts and government spending.[7] These massive and unprecedented interventions show clearly that governments felt they had a role to play in correcting economic crises through direct fiscal and monetary interventions in the economy. Keynes's work remains the core academic text underpinning this belief in government economic interventionism.

Limitations

Keynes's work has had an enormous influence on both the field of economic theory and on politics and broader public policy. More, its importance has not proven to be limited to a specific time period. Instead, Keynesian economics has shown itself relevant to all contexts and economic debates. It provides a coherent theoretical framework for addressing key economic questions such as unemployment, demand, economic growth, and the role of the government in the economy. These are questions that affect all localities and historical periods. The work appears to have relevance to all geographical, temporal, or political contexts.

That said, Keynesian economics has undergone a continuous process of reinterpretation, reinvention, and shift in reputation since *The General Theory*'s publication in 1936. Its ability to survive in the face of these changes is a testament to its strength. As one form of Keynesianism* broke down, a process of academic discussion and debate would produce a newer form of it; following the stagflation* (a term, made up from the words "stagnation" and "inflation," describing the economic phenomenon in which inflation occurs without economic growth) of the 1970s, for example, the mainstream neo-Keynesianism* of the 1950s and 1960s (held by many to be a synthesis of Keynesian and classical economic theory) was replaced by new Keynesian economics.*

This challenged the reemergence of classical economics by providing greater theoretical proof for Keynesian theories. As classical theories evolved in response to new Keynesian economics, Keynesianism itself evolved further, producing the post-Keynesian* school of thought (an interpretation of Keynesian theory which returns, in many ways, to the ideas as they were first set out, rejecting the synthesis with classical economic theory). In short, there now exists a vast literature that tries to explain and develop Keynes's original work.

NOTES

1   Keynes to Shaw, quoted in Johnson Cassidy, "The Demand Doctor," *The New Yorker,* October 10, 2011.

2   *Economist*, "John Maynard Keynes," November 26, 2013, accessed September 14, 2015, http://www.economist.com/blogs/freeexchange/2013/11/keynes-from-the-archives.

3   Letter to the editor, "Friedman & Keynes," *Time*, February 4, 1966.

4   Review and Outlook, "We are All Keynesians Now," *Wall Street Journal*, January 18, 2008, accessed September 14, 2015, http://www.wsj.com/articles/SB120062129547799439.

5   Roger C. Altman, "The Great Crash, 2008: A Geopolitical Setback for the West," *Foreign Affairs*, January/February 2009, accessed September 14, 2015, https://www.foreignaffairs.com/articles/united-states/2009-01-01/great-crash-2008.

6   United States Department of the Treasury, Office of Financial Stability, "Troubled Asset Relief Program: Two Year Retrospective," October 5, 2010, accessed September 14, 2015, http://www.treasury.gov/

initiatives/financial-stability/reports/Documents/TARP%20Two%20Year%20
Retrospective_10%2005%2010_transmittal%20letter.pdf.

7   BBC News, "US Congress passes stimulus plan," February 14,
    2009, accessed September 14, 2015, http://news.bbc.co.uk/2/hi/
    business/7889897.stm.

MODULE 8
PLACE IN THE AUTHOR'S WORK

KEY POINTS

- Keynes's life work was focused on improving government policy and carving out a greater role for government interventions in economic life.

- *The General Theory* represents the key work for understanding Keynes's economic thought and philosophy. It is a synthesis and development of all his previous works.

- *The General Theory* is one of the most important economic texts ever written and the greatest work of its author, John Maynard Keynes.

Positioning

The General Theory of Employment, Interest and Money was the culmination of ideas that Keynes began to examine early in his career, and represents his most radical departure from the ideas of classical economics.* His first book, *Indian Currency and Finance*, was published in 1913. Soon after, Keynes was appointed to the Royal Commission on Indian Finance and Currency—the beginning of a very influential career in public affairs. In 1914, immediately following the outbreak of World War I,* he was called to the British Treasury (the arm of the government tasked with implementing economic policy). By 1919 he was the Treasury's main representative at the Paris Peace Conference* (a meeting called by the war's victors to discuss the implications of defeat for the war's losing nations). His disagreement with decisions regarding reparations (that is, money to be paid in order to make amends) led to his resignation and the writing of his first major work,

> 66 The composition of this book has been for the author a long struggle of escape ... from habitual modes of thought and expression ... The difficulty lies, not in the new ideas, but in escaping from the old ones, which ramify, for those brought up as most of us have been, into every corner of our minds. 99
>
> John Maynard Keynes, *The General Theory of Employment, Interest and Money*

The Economic Consequences of the Peace.[1] During the 1920s Keynes remained a figure of national importance. He opposed the gold standard* (a monetary system in which the standard economic unit is related to the price of gold) and was the author of important publications, such as *A Treatise on Probability* (1921), and *A Tract on Monetary Reform* (1923).[2]

In *A Tract on Monetary Reform* Keynes was already arguing for an increased role for government in economic management, calling for a depreciation (a lessening in value) of the British currency to make exports more competitive and boost manufacturing employment. By 1924 he was calling for direct fiscal intervention in the economy, arguing that the government should undertake public works programs to create jobs.[3] He had little effect on policymaking at the time, however. One commentator suggested this was because the theoretical basis for his assertions was so weak.[4] These nevertheless laid the foundations for many of his ideas in *The General Theory*.

In 1930 he produced *The Treatise on Money*, a book primarily concerned with the factors governing the level of prices. It was, he said, "still moving along the traditional lines of regarding the influence of money as something so to speak separate from the general theory of supply* and demand."[5] However, it also expressed his views on many features of money and the institutional details of the banking system that appeared in his later work. For instance, he began to develop the central idea—so important to *The General Theory*—that the level of savings in an economy can exceed the level of investment, perhaps as a result of excessively high interest rates, and that this can drive unemployment.

In 1933, at the height of the Great Depression,* Keynes published *The Means to Prosperity*, which argued for specific interventionist policies to reduce unemployment. In this text, Keynes first mentioned the concept of "the multiplier effect"* (the increase in the nation's income arising from a new injection of spending into the economy) that he later developed in *The General Theory*. The economic crisis ensured that he now received attention from policymakers in Britain and the United States. This prepared the ground for a greater acceptance of these and other ideas that were synthesized in *The General Theory*.[6]

Integration

The General Theory was the culmination of Keynes's economic thought and philosophy. There is a clear line between his earlier work and *The General Theory*, which is widely considered his most substantial contribution to economics. His goal in publication was to challenge the "classical theory of the subject, upon which I was brought up and which dominates the economic thought, both practical and theoretical, of the governing and academic classes of this generation, as it has for a hundred years past."[7]

Keynes's ideas were formed in response to the economic conditions of his time. He began to criticize the classical understanding of monetary policy in the 1920s, when he witnessed what he believed was blind adherence to the gold standard by the British government. The decision by the then Chancellor of the Exchequer Winston Churchill* to bring Britain back onto the gold standard in 1925, despite the negative impact on British industry due to the appreciation of the pound, led Keynes to publish *The Economic Consequences of Mr. Churchill* (1925). The title was a play on his earlier work, *The Economic Consequences of the Peace*, which predicted disastrous economic consequences for Europe as a direct result of the harsh treaty terms imposed on Germany in the Treaty of Versailles.* These early publications highlighted Keynes's desire to engage directly with the key economic and political questions of his time.

Significance

The emergence of a coherent branch of economic thought, referred to as Keynesianism,* shows the significance of Keynes's work. The birth of this school of thought can be traced to the publication of *The General Theory*, which is why it represents his most important contribution to economics and the culmination of his life's work. The central idea of Keynesianism is the belief that market economies are unstable and require governments to intervene and correct them. *The General Theory* presented economic and theoretical ideas that Keynes had been developing for decades. Its publication during the worst economic crisis on record, the Great Depression, ensured that it received an interested response from policymakers and economists.

Despite the circumstances of its publication, *The General Theory* and the Keynesian school of economic thought have adapted to changing economic circumstances in the decades since publication. From the central economic planning of the postwar period, to the Keynesian stimulus policies of the 1960s, and through the reformation of Keynesian economics following the classical resurgence of the 1970s and 1980s (when a belief in free markets was promoted by US President Ronald Reagan* and British Prime Minister Margaret Thatcher),* Keynesianism has evolved.

The role of Keynesian economics in averting another Great Depression following the 2007–8 financial crisis* shows that the book remains just as relevant today as when it was first published in 1936.[8]

NOTES

1   John Maynard Keynes, *The Economic Consequences of the Peace* (New York: Harcourt, Brace & Howe, 1920).

2   John Maynard Keynes, *A Tract on Monetary Reform* (London: Macmillan, 1923).

3   Robert Skidelsky, *John Maynard Keynes: 1883–1946: Economist, Philosopher, Statesman*. (London: Pan MacMillan, 2003): 217–20, 245, 260–5, 283, 342–55.

4   Hyman Minsky, *John Maynard Keynes* (New York: McGraw-Hill, 2008), chapter 1.

5   John Maynard Keynes, *The General Theory of Employment, Interest and Money*, *The Collected Writings of John Maynard Keynes, Vol 7* (London: Macmillan/St. Martin's Press, 1973), xxi.

6   Skidelsky, *Keynes 1883–1946*, 494–500, 504, 509–10.

7   Keynes, *The General Theory*, 3.

8   Robert Skidelsky, *Keynes: The Return of the Master* (New York: Public Affairs, 2009).

SECTION 3
IMPACT

THE FIRST RESPONSES

KEY POINTS

- *The General Theory* received a relatively warm reception upon publication. Many criticisms have been leveled since. These generally emerged from the ideological battle between Keynesian* and classical* economics.

- Marxists* criticized the work for being too close to classical economics. As Keynes's later supporters argued, however, Keynes's goal was to save capitalism by reforming it.

- The severity and length of the Great Depression* was the main factor that determined reception to the book. The Depression made academics and policymakers more receptive to its ideas.

Criticism

John Maynard Keynes's book *The General Theory of Employment, Interest and Money* was received relatively well on publication. Many of Keynes's early ideas for monetary reforms, works programs, and stimulus policies had been ignored in the 1920s; according to the American economist Hyman Minsky,* this was because his theoretical underpinnings were "muddled."[1] When *The General Theory* was published, however, policymakers in Britain and the US were more receptive to the idea of a more active government role in economic management, particularly in times of recession. Keynes's 1933 book *The Means to Prosperity* had laid much of the groundwork for this, preparing policymakers for the notion of government intervention.[2]

Whereas this earlier work was effectively a set of policy proposals, *The General Theory* provided them with theoretical underpinnings.

> ❝ [A] major set of truly original ideas, such as Keynes's, cannot be received by the academic community and incorporated into the body of established knowledge without running the gauntlet of a barrage of constructive criticism. ❞
>
> Mark Hayes, *The Economics Of Keynes*

Nevertheless, the general view is that it was not until 1939 that Keynes's work, particularly *The General Theory*, began to have a direct influence on US policy process.

During the 1930s, in the US in particular, economists initially rejected the central ideas of Keynes's work. By the outbreak of World War II,* however, a number of international economists had come to embrace them. For example, the American economist Alvin Hansen* was initially skeptical of *The General Theory* and wrote a negative review soon after its publication. In his presidential address to the American Economic Association, he praised Keynes for advocating more government intervention during a recession. He then went on to mentor a number of important students at Harvard University, including Paul Samuelson* and James Tobin,* both eventual Nobel Prize winners. Hansen developed the "IS-LM" model* with John Hicks* to provide a mathematical model for Keynes's ideas. Showing the link between interest rates and output, this became an orthodox method of understanding Keynesian economics.

Although Keynes's work developed a strong following in mainstream economic thought, Marxists and a number of political theorists remained highly critical of it.[3] Although the Marxist historian Paul Sweezy* found much to praise in Keynes's work, he still said it was a fundamentally classical approach to economics and argued that Keynes had overlooked key issues such as the role of class in the capitalist* system.[4] Others argued that the methods outlined by

Keynes would be more likely to be implemented by governments in a political manner than in a rational or technocratic (with strict adherence to theory) one.[5]

Responses

Despite the evolution in thinking among many economists and their embrace of Keynesianism,* detractors remained, and classical economics was slow to recede. Keynes failed to engage in early debates about *The General Theory* as he suffered a heart attack just a year after publication. This resulted in a forced period of rest. Some have suggested that Keynes's ideas were quickly watered down by those looking for consensus with classical economists. They further suggest that models such as the famous "IS-LM" model were a distortion of Keynes's ideas, intended to stop divisions within the discipline.[6] With the outbreak of war, Keynes's intellectual talents were quickly redirected toward assisting the British war effort. He also led postwar economic negotiations with Britain's chief ally, the United States.

Further, he was tasked with helping to design the new international financial order that is often traced to the Bretton Woods Conference* held in the United States following World War II.* He directed much of his energy toward creating a vision for the postwar international order, based on the better management of global capitalism and the use of international economic institutions to increase international cooperation.[7]

Addressing the political feasibility of implementing his policies, Keynes did acknowledge: "The theory of aggregated production, which is the point of the following book, nevertheless can be much easier adapted to the conditions of a totalitarian state ... than the theory of production and distribution of a given production put forth under conditions of free competition and a large degree of laissez-faire."[8] "Laissez-faire" is a French term, meaning a policy of leaving things to take their own course.

Conflict and Consensus

Soon after the war, as he watched Britain's economic situation deteriorate, Keynes did backtrack on his views slightly. Speaking to an advisor to the Bank of England, he suggested that: "I find myself more and more relying for a solution of our problems [on the self-correcting character of an unimpeded free market] which I tried to eject from economic thinking twenty years ago."[9]

It is difficult to know whether this was a genuine retraction of his skepticism about free markets or a reflection of the policy dilemmas he faced. Keynes died in 1946, ten years after the publication of *The General Theory*. Personal health struggles and world events prevented him from engaging in major debates about his work. Instead he left the interpretation and discussion of his text to other economists— debates that continue to the present day.

There remains a divide among economists between Keynesians such as the Nobel Prize-winning American economist Paul Krugman,* who argue for strong government stimulus efforts to jump-start the economy in times of recession, and others, such as Alex Tabarrok,* who argue that Keynesian policies have failed whenever they have been tried. Tabarrok writes that the Great Depression and the 2007–8 financial crisis* were two examples "that massively favored Keynesian economics but Keynesian politics failed both times."[10] He continues, "if we can't count on massive increases in government spending during a recession to mop up problems ex-post shouldn't we all, Keynesians and otherwise, be spending more time thinking about ex-ante alternatives to Keynesian politics?"[11]

NOTES

1   Hyman Minsky, *John Maynard Keynes* (New York: McGraw-Hill, 2008), 1–19.

2   Robert Skidelsky, *John Maynard Keynes: 1883–1946: Economist,*

Philosopher, Statesman. (London: Pan MacMillan, 2003), 494–500, 504, 509–10.

3   Michael Charles Howard and John Edward King, *A History of Marxian Economics, Volume II: 1929–1990*, (Princeton: Princeton University Press), 91–108.

4   P. M. Sweezy, "John Maynard Keynes," *Science and Society* 10, no. 4 (1946): 398–405.

5   James M. Buchanan and Richard E. Wagner, *Democracy in Deficit: The Political Legacy of Lord Keynes* (Indianapolis, IN: Liberty Fund, 1999).

6   Minsky, *John Maynard Keynes.*

7   Donald Markwell, *John Maynard Keynes and International Relations: Economic Paths to War and Peace* (Oxford: Oxford University Press, 2006).

8   Alex Tabarrok, "The Failure of Keynesian Politics," *Marginal Revolution,* February 16, 2011, accessed September 14, 2015, http://marginalrevolution.com/marginalrevolution/2011/02/the-failure-of-keynesian-politics.html.

9   MaynardKeynes.org, "John Maynard Keynes Timeline," accessed September 14, 2015, http://www.maynardkeynes.org/john-maynard-keynes-world-bank-imf.html.

10   Tabarrok, "The Failure of Keynesian Politics."

11   Tabarrok, "The Failure of Keynesian Politics."

MODULE 10
THE EVOLVING DEBATE

KEY POINTS

- Although the key original idea in *The General Theory* has remained intact, its expression and theoretical underpinnings have evolved. This key idea remains— that economies are prone to prolonged troughs (such as periods of high unemployment) that require government intervention.

- A number of schools of thought have emerged as a result. These included orthodox Keynesianism,* new Keynesianism* and post-Keynesianism.*

- The book changed the study and implementation of economics, perhaps more than any other single text. It provided academic support for a drastic expansion of government involvement in the economy.

Uses and Problems

John Maynard Keynes's *The General Theory of Employment, Interest and Money* is an extremely complex book. As one commentator wrote in 1946: "It is a badly written book, poorly organized," but ultimately "a work of genius."[1]

Consequently *The General Theory* has spawned a vast literature that attempts to demystify and explain its conclusions. The first example came in 1937 in an article written by the British economist John Hicks,* entitled "Mr. Keynes and the 'Classics': A Suggested Interpretation."[2] This became Hicks's most famous contribution to the field of economics. In the article, he provided the first formal macroeconomic* model (that is, a large-scale economic model) to represent Keynesian economic theory. It was extended by the American economist Alvin Hansen* in 1953 to become the Hicks-Hansen* model.[3] This suggests that economic outcomes represent a balance between money, consumption, and investment.

It was later widely recognized, not only by Hicks himself, that the model missed important aspects of Keynes's arguments, including those relating to economic uncertainty.[4] The model is still used in economics textbooks, but is understood as a simplification for understanding—not describing—real-world phenomena. It highlighted the difficulty of drawing clear implications and assumptions from Keynes's work and presaged decades of debate and discussion over the means, interpretation, and evolution of Keynesian thought.

Schools of Thought

Keynes's work emerged in opposition to classical* or neoclassical economics* (an approach to economic theory founded on the three propositions that people are rational and have discernible preferences based on value; people maximize utility while firms maximize profits; and people will act independently, given full and relevant information). The "neoclassical synthesis"* emerged after World War II* as an attempt to incorporate Keynes's ideas into neoclassical economics. The result has been a division of postwar economics into two strands. Macroeconomics, or the study of the economy as a whole, is dominated by Keynesian economics. Microeconomics,* or the study of individuals and small organizations in an economy, has been dominated by neoclassical thought.[5]

After World War II, Keynesian economics came to dominate economic policymaking.[6] As the then–US president Richard Nixon* famously said in the early 1970s, "I am now a Keynesian."[7] In the 1970s a series of economic crises, most notably the onset of economic stagnation* coupled with widespread inflation* undermined the faith of policymakers in Keynesian economics. The school of monetarists* led by Milton Friedman* (a school founded on free-market principles, and on the argument that control of the amount of money in circulation is the most effective way to manage an economy), tried to radically reshape the understanding of the economy along classical lines. New classical macroeconomics* began to criticize Keynesian economics by providing a neoclassical microeconomic underpinning for economic analyses.

Following this, the new Keynesian school emerged to provide a more solid microeconomic theoretical foundation for Keynes's work by highlighting examples of market failure*—in particular, the existence of imperfect competition, where regulations or other non-market forces prevent the free market from operating in relation to purely economic forces, and the inability of wages and prices to correct themselves. In particular, new Keynesian economics shows that imperfect competition can make wages and prices "sticky" and not subject to change, thereby sustaining unemployment.

Post-Keynesian economists rejected the neoclassical synthesis and any application of neoclassical economics to the macroeconomy. They argued that neo-Keynesian and new Keynesian economics represented a misinterpretation of Keynes's ideas. Post-Keynesians try to develop the original intent of Keynes's ideas, without using neoclassical models or economics. As Keynes's biographer Robert Skidelsky* argues, post-Keynesians are often seen as following the spirit of Keynes's work most closely. Their influence has been limited, however.[8]

In Current Scholarship

Keynesianism remains one of the main schools of economic thought. The ideas that began with the publication of *The General Theory* have been expanded, debated, reviewed, reformed, renewed, and continued. Economic policymaking has gone through various cycles over the years, but Keynes has cast a long shadow over the field. Even when he was out of favor, for example under the free-market leadership of British Prime Minister Margaret Thatcher* or US President Roland Reagan,* the supporters of classical economics have had to defend against Keynesian criticisms and policy alternatives. Keynes's ideas have survived decades of critique and implementation and remain vital up to the present day, as shown by their widespread adoption after the 2007–8 global financial crisis.*

The phenomenon of the "liquidity trap"* is an example of Keynes's ideas correctly predicting real-world events. Keynes warned that under economic conditions of deflation* (that is, falling prices and wages), additional money injections into the banking system via expansionary monetary policy* could fail to halt the deflationary cycle, as households might simply choose to hoard additional money rather than spend it. John Hicks* incorporated the idea into his famous IS-LM model.* The economist Paul Krugman* wrote in 1998 that the "liquidity trap" idea "played a central role in the early years of macroeconomics as a discipline."[9] In the same year, describing Japan's prolonged economic slump, he said:"It's back."[10]

NOTES

1 P. A. Samuelson, "The General Theory," *Econometrica* 14 (July), Reprinted in H. Lekachman (ed.) *Keynes' General Theory* (New York: St. Martin's Press, [1946] 1964), 316.

2 J. R. Hicks, "Mr. Keynes And The 'Classics'; A Suggested Interpretation," *Econometrica* 5, no. 2 (1937): 147.

3 Alvin H. Hansen, *A Guide To Keynes* (New York: McGraw-Hill, 1953).

4 John Hicks, "'IS-LM': An Explanation," *Journal of Post Keynesian Economics* 3, no. 2 (1980): 139–54.

5 B. Clark, *Political Economy: A Comparative Approach* (Westport, CT: Praeger, 1998).

6 Gordon Fletcher, *The Keynesian Revolution and Its Critics: Issues of Theory and Policy for the Monetary Production Economy* (London: Palgrave MacMillan, 1989), xix–xxi.

7 Review and Outlook, "We are All Keynesians Now," *Wall Street Journal*, January 18, 2008, accessed September 14, 2015, http://www.wsj.com/articles/SB120062129547799439.

8 Robert Skidelsky, *Keynes: The Return of the Master* (New York: Public Affairs, 2009).

9 Paul R. Krugman, "It's Baaack: Japan's Slump and the Return of the Liquidity Trap," *Brookings Papers on Economic Activity 2,* 1998, accessed September 14, 2015, http://www.brookings.edu/~/media/projects/bpea/1998%202/1998b_bpea_krugman_dominquez_rogoff.pdf.

10 Krugman, "It's Baaack."

MODULE 11
IMPACT AND INFLUENCE TODAY

KEY POINTS

- *The General Theory* is widely viewed as one of the most important and relevant economics texts ever written.

- The key challenge remains how to apply Keynes's core insight about the inherent instability of the capitalist* economy to achieve effective government intervention.

- Many who oppose Keynes's ideas believe that government intervention is likely to do more harm than good.

Position

John Maynard Keynes's ideas, presented in *The General Theory of Employment Interest and Money,* had a profound impact on further developments of both theory and practice in modern economics. Following the work, a new field of economic enquiry, "macroeconomics,"* was created. This focuses on the study of aggregate (that is, combined) economic variables, and the determination of output, income, and employment beyond the level of prices in the economic system as a whole.

The interpretations of Keynes's ideas also spawned a vast literature and a new approach to economics—Keynesian* economics. The interpretation and formalization of *The General Theory* presented by the economist John Hicks* in his article "Mr. Keynes and the 'Classics': A Suggested Interpretation" became the commonly accepted view.[1] In his article Hicks introduced what would become regarded in macroeconomic textbooks as the "IS-LM"* framework, which shows the relationship between income and interest rates, and he tried to reconcile Keynes's ideas with the classical* framework. This initial

> ❝ What his book really was about was the proper understanding of the convulsive downturns to which free market economies are intermittently prone. And in that, Keynesians have been vindicated. The core Keynesian lesson, which is that most of the time economies are self-stabilizing, but two or three times a century, they become self-destabilizing, where a worse financial system creates a worse economy creates a worse financial system, has been central to this episode. ❞
>
> "Larry Summers: 'I Think Keynes Mistitled His Book'," *Washington Post*

attempt was developed in the neo-Keynesian* economist Paul Samuelson's* macroeconomics textbook *Economics: an Introductory Analysis*,[2] which spread the main ideas of the Keynesian approach around the academic world. One of the founders of neo-Keynesian economics, Samuelson coined the term "neoclassical synthesis"* to describe the combination of Keynesian and classical principles.

Interaction

The core debate between Keynesians and more classically oriented economists revolves around the efficiency of the free market relative to government intervention and regulation. Those who follow the Keynesian school say that free-market outcomes are often inefficient and that active government policies, both fiscal* and monetary,* are required to correct them. Classical economics maintains that markets are efficient, and warns that active government policies produce unintended consequences that can distort and diminish employment and economic activity (by, for example, generating inflation).*

Current debate is mostly dominated by the new classical* and new Keynesian* approaches, which in turn have either totally confronted or partially overlooked the original ideas developed in *The General Theory*. The main responses to the sort of intervention supported by Keynesianism came from monetarists* and new classical economists. This was particularly in cases where policies of demand management* (according to which the government determines the consumption patterns of individuals and the economy as a whole) based on the Keynesian approach were not preventing economies from registering low rates of economic activity and high rates of inflation, as was true in the 1970s. Their motives were political as much as intellectual, but policymakers around the world subsequently adopted their conclusions.

In the monetarist view, the economy has a tendency to return to its natural rate of output and employment unless disturbed by erratic monetary policy. There is, therefore, no need for policy intervention, since authorities' decisions on the strength of fiscal and monetary policies can do more harm than good.[3]

The new classical school is based on neoclassical* microfoundations* (the behavior of individual agents, such as households or firms, that underpins a macroeconomic theory). It holds the same belief that there is no need for stabilization policy. It assumes that people are rational about market conditions and that markets are not systematically wrong; free-market forces, they assert, deliver economic equilibrium through adjustments in prices and wages. In this framework, money works as a veil where monetary variables (the price of fabric, for example) do not affect real variables (the quantity of T-shirts in a warehouse, for example) since individuals and firms are able to make any economic adjustment in advance, as long as their information is complete. The American economist Robert Lucas* is recognized as the founding father of this school of thought.[4]

The Continuing Debate

The interpretations of Keynes's ideas have given rise to different schools of economic thought. The demise of the mainstream neoclassical synthesis position in the early 1970s created room for the rise and consolidation of two counterrevolutionary approaches— monetarism and the new classical school. Unlike the general Keynesian view, which argues for aggregate demand* management policies to stabilize fluctuations in output and employment, both approaches share the core belief that there is no need for state interventionism in the economy. They returned to the pre-Keynesian belief that the economic system is self-adjusting, unless disturbed by economic policies, and that free-market forces create a natural level of output and employment.

Current macroeconomic debate, however, is mainly dominated by the views of the new classical and the new Keynesian schools. The latter adapts microeconomics* to macroeconomic theory, but the former adapts macroeconomic theory to neoclassical microfoundations.[5]

Post-Keynesian economists, whose ideas can be traced back to the writings of Keynes and his contemporaries or disciples, such as Joan Robinson,* Nicholas Kaldor,* Michal Kalecki,* George Shackle,* and Piero Sraffa,* are a small group whose views stand apart from the mainstream macroeconomics presented in textbooks and taught at most universities nowadays. Despite this, it is worth mentioning that in response to the current financial crisis, ideas in *The General Theory* that have for a long time been misrepresented or overlooked by mainstream macroeconomics have been revived in both the intellectual and practical environment of the discipline.

Issues Keynes mentioned as a response to the Great Depression,[x] such as the unstable character of financial markets, the need for a regulatory framework, and state intervention to stimulate an economy experiencing recession, are once more debated as similar adverse economic conditions arise in the leading capitalist economies.

NOTES

1   John R. Hicks, "Mr. Keynes and the 'Classics': A Suggested Interpretation," *Econometrica* 5, no. 2 (1937): 147–59.

2   Paul A. Samuelson, *Economics: An Introductory Analysis* (New York: McGraw Hill, 1948).

3   Milton Friedman, "The Role of Monetary Policy," *American Economic Review* 58 (1968): 1–17.

4   Robert E. Lucas Jr., *Studies in Business Cycle Theory* (Oxford: Basil Blackwell, 1981).

5   Brian Snowdon and Howard R. Vane, *Modern Macroeconomics: Its origins, Development and Current State* (Cheltenham: Edward Elgar, 2005).

MODULE 12
WHERE NEXT?

KEY POINTS

- *The General Theory* will remain a key text for understanding economics and developing new policies into the coming century.

- The book will serve as a reference point for policymakers in discussing how to manage macroeconomic* (economy-wide) fluctuations and crises.

- The book reshaped the academic and policy study of economics. It forced a systemic rethink of the theoretical foundations of economics and the almost unquestioned belief in the efficiency of free markets.

Potential

John Maynard Keynes's *The General Theory of Employment, Interest and Money* is highly relevant not only to the study of economics, but also to broader policymaking. The 2007–8 financial crisis* sparked a "Keynesian* resurgence."[1] Keynesian policymaking came to the fore in Western policymaking from World War II* through to the 1970s, when presidents and policymakers expressed faith in its new approach to economics.[2] After that, classical* and free-market economic thinking enjoyed a revival, and became dominant in the 1980s as Western governments shied away from active intervention in the economy.

With the onset of the financial crisis in 2007–8 and the perceived risk that the world stood on the brink of another Great Depression,* Western governments have re-embraced proactive Keynesian policies in order to stimulate economic growth and employment, for example

> **❝** [Keynes] was one of the great liberals of our time. He saw clearly that in England and the United States during the nineteen-thirties, the road to serfdom lay, not down the path of too much government control, but down the path of too little, and too late ... He tried to devise the minimum government controls that would allow free enterprise to work. The end of laissez-faire was not necessarily the beginning of communism. **❞**
>
> A. F. W. Plumptre, "Keynes in Cambridge."

by bailing out car companies and banks.

Keynes's work will remain one of the core texts in the discipline of economics. It has fundamentally reshaped the way economists view both their subject and the wider world.

New Keynesianism* focuses on the discussion of microfoundations,* the behavior of individual agents such as households or firms that underpins a macroeconomic theory, as a way of understanding macroeconomic dynamics; examples of microfoundations are price and wage rigidities* (where wages or the price of goods do not change immediately following changes in demand and supply).* Moreover, it generally accepts the new classical* assumption that economic agents have rational expectations, according to which they are able to make economic adjustments in advance, as long as the information they have is complete. In this regard, it differs from Keynes's arguments, especially in rejecting the uncertainty or irrationality of individuals.

Additionally, the proponents of this approach allow for market failures in their models, but argue for more flexibility in wages and prices to reduce unemployment; this is closer to the classical defense that economic systems self-adjust when there is no rigidity, rather than the view Keynes expressed in *The General Theory*. Although theoretically new Keynesianism departs from most of Keynes's ideas, in terms of policy recommendation it does agree with the need for stabilization policies to manage economic fluctuations.[3]

Post-Keynesian* economists place great emphasis on central themes in *The General Theory* that have been mostly overlooked by the standard approach: for example, the special role of money and financial institutions, the instability of capitalist* economies, and the concepts of the money economy and the existence of market uncertainty. They also take a historical view of international issues that Keynes was not concerned about; his primary aim was to provide an alternative understanding of the capitalist economic system and the determination of the level of economic activity, in contrast to the classical framework.

The General Theory provided a basis for many interpretations and further discussion. It raised important issues that moved beyond theoretical analysis and had an actual effect on policymaking. The text has become a key point of reference for both critics and followers of Keynes, who either question or accept and extend the ideas he presented.

Future Directions

The Keynesian economics tradition has produced a number of notable "star" academics and policymakers. It has also provided a spark for many others, who continue to reject proactive government policies and the idea that the free market has inherent weaknesses. Other economists remain somewhere in between. For example, Martin Wolf,* an economist at the *Financial Times*, was quoted after the 2007–8 financial crisis as saying: "I no longer believe in the market's self-healing power."[4]

President Barack Obama* of the United States perhaps best typifies the Keynesian strand in contemporary policymaking. Following the onset of the 2007–8 financial crisis, Obama steered a massive stimulus package through the United States Congress as a means to stimulate employment and economic growth. At the other end of the spectrum is the "Tea Party"* faction of the Republican Party, which rejects any role for the government in managing the economy.

Within the field of economics, the Nobel Prize-winning economist Paul Krugman* remains perhaps the most prominent self-professed Keynesian economist. Following the financial crisis in 2008, he wrote *The Return of Depression Economics and the Crisis of 2008*.[5]

Summary

As one of the most influential works in economics, *The General Theory* was a successful attempt to examine economic problems outside the prevailing classical theoretical framework. The book has long-term importance due to the subsequent developments that it inspired: it revolutionized both economic theory and economic policy recommendations. It argued that the full employment and natural balance of capitalist economies, believed in by classical economists, can only occur in particular cases; it detailed the important role that states should play in boosting aggregate demand* (and therefore economic activity) in order to achieve full employment.

From the aftermath of World War II* through to the 1970s, Keynesian economics ascended to the pinnacle of economic policymaking and became, for a time, almost unchallenged in US and Western Europe. Many attribute the success of Keynesian ideas to the monumental borrowing undertaken by governments to finance the war, and the recognition that it had been the key factor in eliminating unemployment and finally ending the Great Depression.* As the economist John Kenneth Galbraith* commented, "one could not have had a better demonstration of the Keynesian ideas."[6]

NOTES

1 Quinn Bowman, "Keynes' Economic Theories Re-emerge in Government Intervention Policies," *PBS*, February 23, 2009, accessed September 14, 2015, http://www.pbs.org/newshour/updates/business-jan-june09-keynes_02-23/.

2 Review and Outlook, "We are All Keynesians Now," *Wall Street Journal*, January 18, 2008, accessed September 14, 2015, http://www.wsj.com/articles/SB120062129547799439.

3 Brian Snowdon and Howard R. Vane, *Modern Macroeconomics: Its Origins, Development and Current State* (Cheltenham: Edward Elgar, 2005).

4 Martin Wolf, "The rescue of Bear Stearns marks liberalization's limit," *Financial Times,* March 25, 2008, accessed September 14, 2015, http://www.ft.com/cms/s/0/8ced5202-fa94-11dc-aa46-000077b07658.html#axzz3lhx7uydW.

5 Paul R. Krugman, *The Return Of Depression Economics And The Crisis Of 2008* (New York: W.W. Norton, 2009).

6 John Kenneth Galbraith, "Interview," *Commanding Heights, PBS,* 28 September 2000, accessed September 14, 2015, http://www.pbs.org/wgbh/commandingheights/shared/minitext/int_johnkennethgalbraith.html.

GLOSSARY

GLOSSARY OF TERMS

2007–8 financial crisis: an economic crisis that began in the US, and which led to a global economic downturn, widely considered the worst financial crisis since the Wall Street Crash of 1929.

Aggregate demand: the total level of goods and services demanded in an economy at a given time. It consists of household spending on goods (C) + capital investments (I) + government spending (G) + exports (X) – (minus) imports from abroad (M). The standard equation is set out as $AD = C + I + G + (X - M)$,

Austerity: a set of government policies aimed at reducing government deficits, usually by means of a mixture of spending cuts and tax increases.

Bretton Woods Regime: a landmark system for international monetary rules and exchange rate management, established in 1944. It lasted for almost three decades, during which time most of the leading capitalist economies adopted Keynesian economic policies of state interventionism and demand management in order to promote economic growth.

Capitalism: the economic and social system, characteristic of the US and nations following the Western model, in which industry is held in private hands and operates for the sake of private profit.

Carthaginian peace: the imposition of a brutal and crushing peace on a defeated enemy.

Classical economics: a theory that argues that market forces will lead the economy to equilibrium through the price mechanism that will efficiently allocate all available resources.

Communism: an economic and social system founded on the abolition of class and private industry, in which the people own the resources and tools required for production, and profit is shared fairly.

Deflationary spiral: a situation in which falling prices result in falling wages, which result in further falling prices. In this situation, interest rates may lose their ability to stimulate the economy (via lowering), which then becomes stuck in a downward spiral.

Demand: describes a consumer's desire and willingness to purchase a good or service.

Demand management: a situation in which the government determines the consumption patterns of individuals and the economy as a whole.

Economic stagnation: a prolonged absence of economic growth.

Epistemology: the branch of philosophy concerned with the study and theorizing of knowledge and understanding.

Fascism: a radical, right-wing ideology that developed during the twentieth century. Fascism is based on rule by dictatorship and the subjugation of the individual to the state.

Fiscal policy: the use of government spending or taxation to influence the economy.

Full employment: a situation in which all those seeking work can find work.

General glut: an excess of supply in relation to demand.

Global financial crisis 2007–8: a global economic downturn that is widely considered the worst financial crisis since the Great Depression of the 1930s.

Gold standard: a monetary system in which the standard economic unit is related to gold.

Great Depression: the longest and most severe depression of the twentieth century. It originated in the US, with the collapse in stock prices in late 1929. Unemployment in the US reached 25 percent, while other countries saw it rise above 30 percent. In many countries, a prolonged recovery did not occur until the end of World War II.

Inflation: the phenomenon of too much money chasing too few goods causing a rise in the general price level.

IS-LM model/Hicks-Hansen model: a way of examining the interaction between interest rates and the actual output of an economy.

Keynesianism: a school of economic thought that argues that economic markets are not self-correcting. It suggests that proactive government policies can help to stabilize the economy through government spending (fiscal policy) and control of the supply of money (monetary policy).

League of Nations: an international organization created in the aftermath of World War I. It was intended as a forum to resolve international disputes.

Liberalism: a philosophy grounded in ideas of freedom and equality.

It is generally viewed as consisting of two schools: classical liberalism, which places a greater emphasis on liberty, and social liberalism, which places a greater emphasis on equality.

Liquidation policies: policies aimed at massive market corrections by allowing and even encouraging the collapse of existing capital and labor stocks. The economy then reaches a new balance based on demand and supply.

Liquidity trap: a situation where an injection of money into the banking system by a central bank fails to reduce the rate of interest, thereby rendering monetary policy ineffective.

Macroeconomics: the study of the economy as a whole.

Marginal disutility: the negative change in wellbeing (that is, the decrease in happiness) resulting from each additional unit of input. For example, an additional hour worked results in a corresponding loss of leisure time.

Marginal output: the unit of additional output (crops, for example) relative to each unit of additional input (fertilizer, for example).

Marginal product: the change in output (the number of T-shirts, for example) resulting from adding one additional unit of a specific input (a newly-hired sewing machine operator, for example).

Marginal propensity to consume: a metric that quantifies the additional consumption that results from an increase in disposable income.

Marginal utility: a metric that quantifies how much wellbeing is derived from each additional unit of a product consumed.

Market economies: economies in which decisions are based on supply and demand.

Marxism: a political and economic ideology that pursues an analysis of class relations and conflict within society. Founded on the economic and social analysis of the German economist and social theorist Karl Marx, it provides a critique of the development of capitalism and the role of class struggle in economic change.

Marxist economics: a school of economics named after the founding theory of Marxism, from which it is derived.

Market failure: the inability of supply and demand to reach equilibrium, resulting in an inefficient allocation of goods and services.

Microeconomics: the study of how individuals and firms make decisions and allocate their resources based on scarcity.

Microfoundations: the study of individual agents, such as households or firms, that have an overall effect on the economy.

Monetarism: a set of policies based on free-market economics, which suggests that the role of the government is to keep tight control on the amount of money in circulation. Its most famous proponent was Milton Friedman.

Monetary policy: the mechanism used to control the supply of money. A policy that increases the money supply is generally described as expansionary while a policy that decreases the money supply is described as contractionary.

Multiplier effect: refers to the increase in the overall income of the economy that results from any new spending.

Neoclassical economics: a school of economics that constructs its understanding of markets and resource allocation based on three core assumptions: that people are rational and have discernible preferences based on value; that people maximize wellbeing while firms maximize profits; and that people have access to full and relevant information.

Neoclassical synthesis: a school of economics that attempts to join the macroeconomic thinking of John Maynard Keynes with the ideas of neoclassical economics.

New classical economics: a school of economics built upon a neoclassical framework, which constructs its understanding of markets and resource allocation on three core assumptions: that people are rational and have discernible preferences based on value; that people maximize wellbeing while firms maximize profits; that people have access to full and relevant information.

Neo-Keynesianism: a school of Keynesianism that emerged in the post-World War II era. It sought to provide an interpretive basis for Keynes's ideas and formalize many of his thoughts into models previously associated with classical economics. It is also often referred to as the neo-classical synthesis. It came to dominate mainstream economic thought in the 1950s and 1960s.

New Keynesian economics: a school of Keynesianism that emerged following the oil shocks and stagflation of the 1970s. These economic crises undermined the belief in the postwar neoclassical synthesis. New Keynesian economics helped further the theoretical underpinnings of Keynesianism and helped produce the "new neoclassical synthesis."

Nominal wages: wages that do not take into account that the price of goods increases through the process of inflation.

Paris Peace Conference: the meeting of the victorious allies after World War I. It determined the peace terms that would be imposed on the defeated nations.

Post-Keynesian economics: school of Keynesian economics that rejects the neoclassical synthesis and any application of neoclassical economics to the macroeconomy. It attempts to go back to what Keynes originally meant, and views later interpretations as being watered down to fit with neoclassical ideas.

Price and wage rigidities: a situation in which wages or the price of a good do not change immediately after shifts in the demand and supply curve.

Quantity theory of money: in general terms, this theory states that money supply has a direct and proportional relationship to price level. As money is only a means of exchange, it does not affect real variables, such as output and employment, so an increase in the money supply is translated into a rise in prices (that is, the process of inflation).

Real exchange economy: an economy based on the exchange and barter of real commodities, rather than mechanisms for transaction, such as money.

Real wage rate: the wage rate adjusted for inflation.

Ricardian economics/theory: the economic theories derived from the writings of David Ricardo, an English economist born in 1772.

Say's Law: an economic rule, named after the French economist Jean Baptiste Say, that argues that supply is the source of demand in the economy.

Socialism: a political and economic system that aims toward social control of the means of production.

Stagflation: a phenomenon whereby economic stagnation occurs at the same time as rising prices (inflation).

Supply: the total amount of a specific good or service that is available to consumers.

Tea Party: a wing of the US Republican Party that advocates a minimalist role for government and a reduction in the societal tax burden.

Treaty of Versailles: the treaty that determined the peace terms to be imposed on the defeated nations at the end of World War I.

Wall Street Crash: the stock market crash of October 1929 that was widely viewed as pushing the world towards the Great Depression.

World War I: a global conflict, centered in Europe, that began in July 1914 and lasted until November 1918.

World War II: a global conflict from 1939 to 1945 between the Allies (Great Britain, the United States, and aligned nations) and the Axis powers (Nazi Germany, Japan, and aligned nations) that saw battles all over the globe.

PEOPLE MENTIONED IN THE TEXT

Winston Churchill (1874–1965) was a British politician who became Prime Minister during World War II.

Francis Edgeworth (1845–1926) was a professor of political economy at the University of Oxford who made significant contributions to statistics and classical economics.

Milton Friedman (1912–2006) was an American economist and a recipient of the 1976 Nobel Prize in Economics. He was a founding figure in the monetarist school of economic thought, and one of the leading intellectual voices of the twentieth century.

John Kenneth Galbraith (1908–2006) was a Canadian and American economist, public official, and diplomat.

Alvin Hansen (1887–1975) was an American economist based at Harvard University.

Friedrich von Hayek (1899–1992) was an Austrian and British economist best known for his work defending classical liberalism.

John Hicks (1904–89) was a British economist mostly based at Oxford University. He was renowned for the influence he had on Keynesian economics and the contribution of his book *Value and Capital* (1939) to the theory of value and the general equilibrium theory.

Herbert Hoover (1874–1964) was the 31st president of the United States. He presided over much of the Great Depression.

Nicholas Kaldor (1908–86) was a Hungarian economist based at Cambridge University, who made special contributions to the study of economic growth.

Michal Kalecki (1899–1970) was a Polish economist who spent part of his life at Cambridge University. His work mainly focused on macroeconomic dynamics and fluctuations in trade cycles.

Florence Ada Keynes (1861–1958) was a social reformer, one of the first women students at Cambridge University, and the first woman mayor of Cambridge. She was John Maynard Keynes's mother.

John Neville Keynes (1852–1949) was an economist and senior administrator of the University of Cambridge, and John Maynard Keynes's father.

Paul Krugman (b. 1953) is an American economist and a professor of economics and international affairs at Princeton University.

Robert Lucas Jr. (b. 1937) is an American economist based at the University of Chicago.

Axel Leijonhufvud (b. 1933) was born in Sweden. He is a professor of economics at the University of California, Los Angeles.

Thomas Malthus (1766–1834) was an influential British scholar in the fields of political economy and demography.

Alfred Marshall (1842–1924) was an important British economist based at Cambridge University and author of the *Principles of Economics*, an influential book that put the ideas of supply and demand, marginal utility, and costs of production into a coherent framework of classical economics.

Karl Marx (1818–83) was a revolutionary German thinker, philosopher, economist, sociologist, and historian. Author of *The Communist Manifesto* and *Capital*, his theories focused on the relationship between labor and capital, and gave rise to Marxism.

Andrew W. Mellon (1855–1937) was an American diplomat and former treasury secretary during the administration of Herbert Hoover.

Hyman Minsky (1919–96) was an American economist whose main contributions were based on Keynes's works, particularly addressing the instability of financial markets and the inherently unstable character of capitalist economies.

James Mill (1773–1836) was a Scottish economist, historian, philosopher, and political theorist who, together with David Ricardo, gave rise to classical economics.

John Stuart Mill (1806–73), the son of James Mill, was a British philosopher and political economist. He was one of the most influential proponents of liberalism, a political philosophy based on the ideas of liberty and equality.

Richard Nixon (1913–94) was the 37th president of the United States, who served from 1969–74.

Barack Obama (b. 1961) is the 44th president of the United States.

Arthur Pigou (1877–1959) was a British economist based at Cambridge University who shared the dominant classical view.

David Ricardo (1772–1823) was an influential British political economist. Author of *On the Principles of Political Economy and Taxation*, he argued in favor of free-market policies and was the founder of classical economics, also known as Ricardian economics, together with James Mill.

Ronald Reagan (1911–2004) was the 40th president of the United States and a strong proponent of free markets.

Joan Robinson (1903–83) was an economist who made important contributions to the study of economic growth and capital accumulation.

Jean Baptiste Say (1767–1832) was a French economist who is considered one of the founding members of the classical school of economics.

George Bernard Shaw (1856–1950) was an Irish playwright, socialist, Keynes's friend, and co-founder of the London School of Economics and Political Science.

George Shackle (1903–92) was a British economist whose works focused on uncertainty and the limitations of knowledge.

Paul Samuelson (1915–2009) was a highly influential American Keynesian academic economist.

Robert Skidelsky (b. 1939) is a British economic historian and Keynesian biographer.

Adam Smith (1723–90) is widely viewed as the father of modern economics. His most notable works are *The Theory of Moral Sentiments*

(1759), and *An Inquiry into the Nature and Causes of the Wealth of Nations* (1776).

Piero Sraffa (1898–1983) was an Italian economist based at Cambridge University whose work *Production of Commodities by Means of Commodities* (1960) was considered a starting point for the neo-Ricardian school of thought.

Paul Sweezy (1910–2004) was a Marxist economist and political activist.

Alex Tabarrok (b. 1966) is an American economist and public intellectual.

Margaret Thatcher (1925–2013) was prime minister of the United Kingdom from 1975–90. She is widely viewed as a champion of free-market ideology.

James Tobin (1918–2002) was an American economist based at Harvard and Yale Universities.

Martin Wolf (b. 1946) is a widely cited and read financial commentator who works for the *Financial Times* newspaper.

WORKS CITED

WORKS CITED

Altman, Roger C. "The Great Crash, 2008." *Foreign Affairs,* January/February 2009. Accessed September 9, 2015. https://www.foreignaffairs.com/articles/united-states/2009–01–01/great-crash-2008.

BBC News. "US Congress Passes Stimulus Plan." February 14, 2009. Accessed September 9, 2015. http://news.bbc.co.uk/2/hi/business/7889897.stm

Bernanke, Ben and Robert H. Frank. *Principles of Microeconomics.* Boston: McGraw-Hill/Irwin, 2007.

Bowman, Quinn. "Keynes' Economic Theories Re-emerge in Government Intervention Policies." PBS, February 23, 2009. Accessed September 9, 2015. http://www.pbs.org/newshour/updates/business-jan-june09-keynes_02-23/.

Buchanan, James M. and Richard E. Wagner. *Democracy in Deficit: The Political Legacy of Lord Keynes.* Indianapolis, IN: Liberty Fund, Inc, 1999.

Cassidy, Johnson. "The Demand Doctor." *The New Yorker*, October 10, 2011. http://www.newyorker.com/magazine/2011/10/10/the-demand-doctor

Clark, B. *Political Economy: A Comparative Approach.* Westport, CT: Praeger, 1998.

Clower, Robert W. "5: Trashing J. B. Say: The Story of a Mare's Nest." In *Macroeconomic Theory and Economic Policy: Essays in Honour of Jean-Paul Fitoussi* by Vela K. Velupillai. London: Routledge, 2004.

De Long, J. Bradford. "'Liquidation' Cycles: Old-Fashioned Real Business Cycle Theory and the Great Depression." National Bureau of Economic Research, Working Paper No. 3546 (1990): 1–37.

Economist. "John Maynard Keynes." November 26, 2013. Accessed September 9, 2015. http://www.economist.com/blogs/freeexchange/2013/11/keynes-from-the-archives.

Fletcher, Gordon. *The Keynesian Revolution and Its Critics: Issues of Theory and Policy for the Monetary Production Economy.* London: Palgrave MacMillan, 1989.

Friedman, Milton. "The Role of Monetary Policy." *American Economic Review* 58, no. 1 (1968): 1–17.

Galbraith, John Kenneth. "Interview." *Commanding Heights, PBS,* September 28, 2000. Accessed September 11, 2015. http://www.pbs.org/wgbh/commandingheights/shared/minitext/int_johnkennethgalbraith.html.

Google Scholar. "John Maynard Keynes, The General Theory of Employment, Interest and Money." Accessed September 14, 2015. https://scholar.google.com/citations?view_op=view_citation&hl=de&user=viLe5BEAAAAJ&citation_for_view=viLe5BEAAAAJ:bFI3QPDXJZMC.

Hansen, Alvin. *A Guide to Keynes*. New York: McGraw Hill, 1953.

_____. *Monetary Theory and Fiscal policy*. New York: McGraw Hill, 1949.

Hayes, Mark. *The Economics Of Keynes*. Cheltenham, UK: Edward Elgar, 2006.

Hicks, John R. "'IS-LM': An Explanation." *Journal of Post Keynesian Economics* 3, no. 2 (1980): 139–54.

_____. "Mr. Keynes and the 'Classics'; a suggested interpretation." *Econometrica* 5, no. 2 (1937): 147–59.

Hoover, Herbert. *The Memoirs of Herbert Hoover, Volume 3: The Great Depression*. New York: The Macmillan Company, 1952. Accessed September 9, 2015. http://www.ecommcode.com/hoover/ebooks/pdf/FULL/B1V3_Full.pdf.

Howard, Michael Charles and King, John Edward. *A History of Marxian Economics, Volume II: 1929–1990*. Princeton: Princeton University Press: 91–108.

Kalecki, Michal. "The Determinants of Distribution of the National Income." *Econometrica* 6, no 2 (1938): 97–112.

Keynes, John Maynard. *A Tract on Monetary Reform*. London: Macmillan, 1923.

_____. *The Economic Consequences of the Peace*. New York: Harcourt Brace, 1920.

_____. "A Monetary Theory of Production." In *The Collected Writings of John Maynard Keynes, Volume 13*. Edited by Austin Robinson and Donald Moggridge. Cambridge: Cambridge University Press for the Royal Economic Society, 2013.

_____. "The Means to Prosperity" *The Collected Writings of John Maynard Keynes, Volume 9*. Edited by Austin Robinson and Donald Moggridge. Cambridge: Cambridge University Press for the Royal Economic Society, 2013.

_____. "The Multiplier." in an edition of "The Means to Prosperity."

_____. "Thomas Robert Malthus: The First of the Cambridge Economists" *The Collected Writings of John Maynard Keynes, Volume 10*. Edited by Austin Robinson and Donald Moggridge. Cambridge: Cambridge University Press for the Royal Economic Society, 2013.

_____. "The Distinction Between a Co-operative Economy and an

Entrepreneur Economy." In *The Collected Writings of John Maynard Keynes, Volume 29*. Edited by Austin Robinson and Donald Moggridge. Cambridge: Cambridge University Press for the Royal Economic Society, 2013.

_____. "The General Theory of Employment." *Quarterly Journal of Economics* 51 (1937): 209–23.

_____. *The General Theory of Employment, Interest and Money*. In *The Collected Writings of John Maynard Keynes, Volume 7*. London: Macmillan/St. Martin's Press, 1973.

_____. *The General Theory Of Employment, Interest, And Money*. Introduced by Paul R. Krugman. Basingstoke, Hampshire: Palgrave Macmillan, 2007.

Klein, Ezra. "Larry Summers: 'I think Keynes mistitled his book.'" *The Washington Post*, July 26, 2011. Accessed September 11, 2015. http://www.washingtonpost.com/blogs/wonkblog/post/larry-summers-i-think-keynes-mistitled-his-book/2011/07/11/glQAzZd4al_blog.html

Krugman, Paul. "It's Baaack: Japan's Slump and the Return of the Liquidity Trap." *Brookings*, 1998. Accessed September 11, 2015. http://www.brookings.edu/~/media/projects/bpea/1998%202/1998b_bpea_krugman_dominquez_rogoff.pdf.

_____. *The Return Of Depression Economics And The Crisis Of 2008*. New York: W.W. Norton, 2009.

_____. "Plutocracy, Paralysis, Perplexity." *The New York Times*, May 3, 2012. http://www.nytimes.com/2012/05/04/opinion/krugman-plutocracy-paralysis-perplexity.html?_r=0

Leijonhufvud, Axel. *On Keynesian Economics and the Economics of Keynes*. London: Oxford University Press, 1968.

_____. *Studies in Business Cycle Theory*. Oxford: Basil Blackwell, 1981.

Mantoux, Etienne. *The Carthaginian Peace: Or the Economic Consequences of Mr Keynes*. Oxford: Oxford University Press, 1946.

Markwell, Donald. *John Maynard Keynes and International Relations: Economic Paths to War and Peace*. Oxford: Oxford University Press, 2006.

MaynardKeynes.org, "John Maynard Keynes Timeline," accessed September 14, 2015, http://www.maynardkeynes.org/john-maynard-keynes-world-bank-imf.html

Mini, Piero V. *John Maynard Keynes*. London: Palgrave Macmillan, 1994.

Minsky, Hyman P. *John Maynard Keynes*. New York: McGraw Hill, 2008.

Pigou, A. C. *The Theory Of Unemployment*. London: Macmillan, 1933.

Samuelson, Paul A. *Economics: An Introductory Analysis*. New York: McGraw Hill, 1948.

_____. "Keynesian Economics and Harvard: in the beginning." *Challenge* July-August (1988): 32–4.

Samuelson, P. A. "The General Theory." *Econometrica* 14 (July). Reprinted in H. Lekachman (ed.) *Keynes' General Theory*. New York: St. Martin's Press, [1946] 1964.

Skidelsky, Robert. *John Maynard Keynes: 1883–1946: Economist, Philosopher, Statesman*. London: Pan MacMillan, 2003.

_____. *John Maynard Keynes: Hopes Betrayed, 1883–1920*. London: Macmillan, 1983.

_____. *Keynes: The Return of the Master*. New York: Public Affairs, 2009.

Snowdon, Brian and Howard R. Vane. *Modern Macroeconomics: Its Origins, Development and Current State*. Cheltenham: Edward Elgar, 2005.

Sweezy, P. M. "John Maynard Keynes." *Science and Society* 10 (1946): 398–405.

Tabarrok, Alex. "The Failure of Keynesian Politics." *Marginal Revolution,* February 16, 2011. Accessed September 11, 2015. http://marginalrevolution. com/marginalrevolution/2011/02/the-failure-of-keynesian-politics.html.

Thies, Clifford F. "The Paradox of Thrift: RIP." *Cato Journal*, 16, no. 1 (1996): 119–27.

Time. "All-Time 100 Nonfiction Books." August 30, 2011. Accessed September 11, 2015. http://entertainment.time.com/2011/08/30/all-time-100-best-nonfiction-books/

_____. "Friedman & Keynes." February 4, 1966.

Tobin, James. "Liquidity Preference as Behavior Towards Risk." *Review of Economic Studies* 25, no. 1 (1958): 65–86.

Unger, Roberto Mangabeira. *Free Trade Reimagined: The World Division of Labor and the Method of Economics*. Princeton: Princeton University Press, 2007.

United States Department of the Treasury: Office of Financial Stability. "Troubled Asset Relief Program: Two Year Retrospective." October 5, 2010. Accessed September 11, 2015. http://www.treasury.gov/initiatives/financial-stability/reports/Documents/TARP%20Two%20Year%20Retrospective_10%20 05%2010_transmittal%20letter.pdf

Wall Street Journal. "We Are All Keynesians Now." January 18, 2008. Accessed September 11, 2015. http://www.wsj.com/articles/SB120062129547799439.

Wolf, Martin. "The rescue of Bear Stearns marks liberalization's limit." *Financial Times,* March 25, 2008. Accessed September 11, 2015. http://www.ft.com/cms/s/0/8ced5202-fa94-11dc-aa46-000077b07658.html#axzz3lRECZApM.

THE MACAT LIBRARY
BY DISCIPLINE

AFRICANA STUDIES

Chinua Achebe's *An Image of Africa: Racism in Conrad's Heart of Darkness*
W. E. B. Du Bois's *The Souls of Black Folk*
Zora Neale Huston's *Characteristics of Negro Expression*
Martin Luther King Jr's *Why We Can't Wait*
Toni Morrison's *Playing in the Dark: Whiteness in the American Literary Imagination*

ANTHROPOLOGY

Arjun Appadurai's *Modernity at Large: Cultural Dimensions of Globalisation*
Philippe Ariès's *Centuries of Childhood*
Franz Boas's *Race, Language and Culture*
Kim Chan & Renée Mauborgne's *Blue Ocean Strategy*
Jared Diamond's *Guns, Germs & Steel: the Fate of Human Societies*
Jared Diamond's *Collapse: How Societies Choose to Fail or Survive*
E. E. Evans-Pritchard's *Witchcraft, Oracles and Magic Among the Azande*
James Ferguson's *The Anti-Politics Machine*
Clifford Geertz's *The Interpretation of Cultures*
David Graeber's *Debt: the First 5000 Years*
Karen Ho's *Liquidated: An Ethnography of Wall Street*
Geert Hofstede's *Culture's Consequences: Comparing Values, Behaviors, Institutes and Organizations across Nations*
Claude Lévi-Strauss's *Structural Anthropology*
Jay Macleod's *Ain't No Makin' It: Aspirations and Attainment in a Low-Income Neighborhood*
Saba Mahmood's *The Politics of Piety: The Islamic Revival and the Feminist Subject*
Marcel Mauss's *The Gift*

BUSINESS

Jean Lave & Etienne Wenger's *Situated Learning*
Theodore Levitt's *Marketing Myopia*
Burton G. Malkiel's *A Random Walk Down Wall Street*
Douglas McGregor's *The Human Side of Enterprise*
Michael Porter's *Competitive Strategy: Creating and Sustaining Superior Performance*
John Kotter's *Leading Change*
C. K. Prahalad & Gary Hamel's *The Core Competence of the Corporation*

CRIMINOLOGY

Michelle Alexander's *The New Jim Crow: Mass Incarceration in the Age of Colorblindness*
Michael R. Gottfredson & Travis Hirschi's *A General Theory of Crime*
Richard Herrnstein & Charles A. Murray's *The Bell Curve: Intelligence and Class Structure in American Life*
Elizabeth Loftus's *Eyewitness Testimony*
Jay Macleod's *Ain't No Makin' It: Aspirations and Attainment in a Low-Income Neighborhood*
Philip Zimbardo's *The Lucifer Effect*

ECONOMICS

Janet Abu-Lughod's *Before European Hegemony*
Ha-Joon Chang's *Kicking Away the Ladder*
David Brion Davis's *The Problem of Slavery in the Age of Revolution*
Milton Friedman's *The Role of Monetary Policy*
Milton Friedman's *Capitalism and Freedom*
David Graeber's *Debt: the First 5000 Years*
Friedrich Hayek's *The Road to Serfdom*
Karen Ho's *Liquidated: An Ethnography of Wall Street*

The Macat Library By Discipline

John Maynard Keynes's *The General Theory of Employment, Interest and Money*
Charles P. Kindleberger's *Manias, Panics and Crashes*
Robert Lucas's *Why Doesn't Capital Flow from Rich to Poor Countries?*
Burton G. Malkiel's *A Random Walk Down Wall Street*
Thomas Robert Malthus's *An Essay on the Principle of Population*
Karl Marx's *Capital*
Thomas Piketty's *Capital in the Twenty-First Century*
Amartya Sen's *Development as Freedom*
Adam Smith's *The Wealth of Nations*
Nassim Nicholas Taleb's *The Black Swan: The Impact of the Highly Improbable*
Amos Tversky's & Daniel Kahneman's *Judgment under Uncertainty: Heuristics and Biases*
Mahbub Ul Haq's *Reflections on Human Development*
Max Weber's *The Protestant Ethic and the Spirit of Capitalism*

FEMINISM AND GENDER STUDIES

Judith Butler's *Gender Trouble*
Simone De Beauvoir's *The Second Sex*
Michel Foucault's *History of Sexuality*
Betty Friedan's *The Feminine Mystique*
Saba Mahmood's *The Politics of Piety: The Islamic Revival and the Feminist Subject*
Joan Wallach Scott's *Gender and the Politics of History*
Mary Wollstonecraft's *A Vindication of the Rights of Woman*
Virginia Woolf's *A Room of One's Own*

GEOGRAPHY

The Brundtland Report's *Our Common Future*
Rachel Carson's *Silent Spring*
Charles Darwin's *On the Origin of Species*
James Ferguson's *The Anti-Politics Machine*
Jane Jacobs's *The Death and Life of Great American Cities*
James Lovelock's *Gaia: A New Look at Life on Earth*
Amartya Sen's *Development as Freedom*
Mathis Wackernagel & William Rees's *Our Ecological Footprint*

HISTORY

Janet Abu-Lughod's *Before European Hegemony*
Benedict Anderson's *Imagined Communities*
Bernard Bailyn's *The Ideological Origins of the American Revolution*
Hanna Batatu's *The Old Social Classes And The Revolutionary Movements Of Iraq*
Christopher Browning's *Ordinary Men: Reserve Police Batallion 101 and the Final Solution in Poland*
Edmund Burke's *Reflections on the Revolution in France*
William Cronon's *Nature's Metropolis: Chicago And The Great West*
Alfred W. Crosby's *The Columbian Exchange*
Hamid Dabashi's *Iran: A People Interrupted*
David Brion Davis's *The Problem of Slavery in the Age of Revolution*
Nathalie Zemon Davis's *The Return of Martin Guerre*
Jared Diamond's *Guns, Germs & Steel: the Fate of Human Societies*
Frank Dikotter's *Mao's Great Famine*
John W Dower's *War Without Mercy: Race And Power In The Pacific War*
W. E. B. Du Bois's *The Souls of Black Folk*
Richard J. Evans's *In Defence of History*
Lucien Febvre's *The Problem of Unbelief in the 16th Century*
Sheila Fitzpatrick's *Everyday Stalinism*

Eric Foner's *Reconstruction: America's Unfinished Revolution, 1863-1877*
Michel Foucault's *Discipline and Punish*
Michel Foucault's *History of Sexuality*
Francis Fukuyama's *The End of History and the Last Man*
John Lewis Gaddis's *We Now Know: Rethinking Cold War History*
Ernest Gellner's *Nations and Nationalism*
Eugene Genovese's *Roll, Jordan, Roll: The World the Slaves Made*
Carlo Ginzburg's *The Night Battles*
Daniel Goldhagen's *Hitler's Willing Executioners*
Jack Goldstone's *Revolution and Rebellion in the Early Modern World*
Antonio Gramsci's *The Prison Notebooks*
Alexander Hamilton, John Jay & James Madison's *The Federalist Papers*
Christopher Hill's *The World Turned Upside Down*
Carole Hillenbrand's *The Crusades: Islamic Perspectives*
Thomas Hobbes's *Leviathan*
Eric Hobsbawm's *The Age Of Revolution*
John A. Hobson's *Imperialism: A Study*
Albert Hourani's *History of the Arab Peoples*
Samuel P. Huntington's *The Clash of Civilizations and the Remaking of World Order*
C. L. R. James's *The Black Jacobins*
Tony Judt's *Postwar: A History of Europe Since 1945*
Ernst Kantorowicz's *The King's Two Bodies: A Study in Medieval Political Theology*
Paul Kennedy's *The Rise and Fall of the Great Powers*
Ian Kershaw's *The "Hitler Myth": Image and Reality in the Third Reich*
John Maynard Keynes's *The General Theory of Employment, Interest and Money*
Charles P. Kindleberger's *Manias, Panics and Crashes*
Martin Luther King Jr's *Why We Can't Wait*
Henry Kissinger's *World Order: Reflections on the Character of Nations and the Course of History*
Thomas Kuhn's *The Structure of Scientific Revolutions*
Georges Lefebvre's *The Coming of the French Revolution*
John Locke's *Two Treatises of Government*
Niccolò Machiavelli's *The Prince*
Thomas Robert Malthus's *An Essay on the Principle of Population*
Mahmood Mamdani's *Citizen and Subject: Contemporary Africa And The Legacy Of Late Colonialism*
Karl Marx's *Capital*
Stanley Milgram's *Obedience to Authority*
John Stuart Mill's *On Liberty*
Thomas Paine's *Common Sense*
Thomas Paine's *Rights of Man*
Geoffrey Parker's *Global Crisis: War, Climate Change and Catastrophe in the Seventeenth Century*
Jonathan Riley-Smith's *The First Crusade and the Idea of Crusading*
Jean-Jacques Rousseau's *The Social Contract*
Joan Wallach Scott's *Gender and the Politics of History*
Theda Skocpol's *States and Social Revolutions*
Adam Smith's *The Wealth of Nations*
Timothy Snyder's *Bloodlands: Europe Between Hitler and Stalin*
Sun Tzu's *The Art of War*
Keith Thomas's *Religion and the Decline of Magic*
Thucydides's *The History of the Peloponnesian War*
Frederick Jackson Turner's *The Significance of the Frontier in American History*
Odd Arne Westad's *The Global Cold War: Third World Interventions And The Making Of Our Times*

The Macat Library By Discipline

LITERATURE

Chinua Achebe's *An Image of Africa: Racism in Conrad's Heart of Darkness*
Roland Barthes's *Mythologies*
Homi K. Bhabha's *The Location of Culture*
Judith Butler's *Gender Trouble*
Simone De Beauvoir's *The Second Sex*
Ferdinand De Saussure's *Course in General Linguistics*
T. S. Eliot's *The Sacred Wood: Essays on Poetry and Criticism*
Zora Neale Huston's *Characteristics of Negro Expression*
Toni Morrison's *Playing in the Dark: Whiteness in the American Literary Imagination*
Edward Said's *Orientalism*
Gayatri Chakravorty Spivak's *Can the Subaltern Speak?*
Mary Wollstonecraft's *A Vindication of the Rights of Women*
Virginia Woolf's *A Room of One's Own*

PHILOSOPHY

Elizabeth Anscombe's *Modern Moral Philosophy*
Hannah Arendt's *The Human Condition*
Aristotle's *Metaphysics*
Aristotle's *Nicomachean Ethics*
Edmund Gettier's *Is Justified True Belief Knowledge?*
Georg Wilhelm Friedrich Hegel's *Phenomenology of Spirit*
David Hume's *Dialogues Concerning Natural Religion*
David Hume's *The Enquiry for Human Understanding*
Immanuel Kant's *Religion within the Boundaries of Mere Reason*
Immanuel Kant's *Critique of Pure Reason*
Søren Kierkegaard's *The Sickness Unto Death*
Søren Kierkegaard's *Fear and Trembling*
C. S. Lewis's *The Abolition of Man*
Alasdair MacIntyre's *After Virtue*
Marcus Aurelius's *Meditations*
Friedrich Nietzsche's *On the Genealogy of Morality*
Friedrich Nietzsche's *Beyond Good and Evil*
Plato's *Republic*
Plato's *Symposium*
Jean-Jacques Rousseau's *The Social Contract*
Gilbert Ryle's *The Concept of Mind*
Baruch Spinoza's *Ethics*
Sun Tzu's *The Art of War*
Ludwig Wittgenstein's *Philosophical Investigations*

POLITICS

Benedict Anderson's *Imagined Communities*
Aristotle's *Politics*
Bernard Bailyn's *The Ideological Origins of the American Revolution*
Edmund Burke's *Reflections on the Revolution in France*
John C. Calhoun's *A Disquisition on Government*
Ha-Joon Chang's *Kicking Away the Ladder*
Hamid Dabashi's *Iran: A People Interrupted*
Hamid Dabashi's *Theology of Discontent: The Ideological Foundation of the Islamic Revolution in Iran*
Robert Dahl's *Democracy and its Critics*
Robert Dahl's *Who Governs?*
David Brion Davis's *The Problem of Slavery in the Age of Revolution*

Alexis De Tocqueville's *Democracy in America*
James Ferguson's *The Anti-Politics Machine*
Frank Dikotter's *Mao's Great Famine*
Sheila Fitzpatrick's *Everyday Stalinism*
Eric Foner's *Reconstruction: America's Unfinished Revolution, 1863-1877*
Milton Friedman's *Capitalism and Freedom*
Francis Fukuyama's *The End of History and the Last Man*
John Lewis Gaddis's *We Now Know: Rethinking Cold War History*
Ernest Gellner's *Nations and Nationalism*
David Graeber's *Debt: the First 5000 Years*
Antonio Gramsci's *The Prison Notebooks*
Alexander Hamilton, John Jay & James Madison's *The Federalist Papers*
Friedrich Hayek's *The Road to Serfdom*
Christopher Hill's *The World Turned Upside Down*
Thomas Hobbes's *Leviathan*
John A. Hobson's *Imperialism: A Study*
Samuel P. Huntington's *The Clash of Civilizations and the Remaking of World Order*
Tony Judt's *Postwar: A History of Europe Since 1945*
David C. Kang's *China Rising: Peace, Power and Order in East Asia*
Paul Kennedy's *The Rise and Fall of Great Powers*
Robert Keohane's *After Hegemony*
Martin Luther King Jr.'s *Why We Can't Wait*
Henry Kissinger's *World Order: Reflections on the Character of Nations and the Course of History*
John Locke's *Two Treatises of Government*
Niccolò Machiavelli's *The Prince*
Thomas Robert Malthus's *An Essay on the Principle of Population*
Mahmood Mamdani's *Citizen and Subject: Contemporary Africa And The Legacy Of Late Colonialism*
Karl Marx's *Capital*
John Stuart Mill's *On Liberty*
John Stuart Mill's *Utilitarianism*
Hans Morgenthau's *Politics Among Nations*
Thomas Paine's *Common Sense*
Thomas Paine's *Rights of Man*
Thomas Piketty's *Capital in the Twenty-First Century*
Robert D. Putman's *Bowling Alone*
John Rawls's *Theory of Justice*
Jean-Jacques Rousseau's *The Social Contract*
Theda Skocpol's *States and Social Revolutions*
Adam Smith's *The Wealth of Nations*
Sun Tzu's *The Art of War*
Henry David Thoreau's *Civil Disobedience*
Thucydides's *The History of the Peloponnesian War*
Kenneth Waltz's *Theory of International Politics*
Max Weber's *Politics as a Vocation*
Odd Arne Westad's *The Global Cold War: Third World Interventions And The Making Of Our Times*

POSTCOLONIAL STUDIES

Roland Barthes's *Mythologies*
Frantz Fanon's *Black Skin, White Masks*
Homi K. Bhabha's *The Location of Culture*
Gustavo Gutiérrez's *A Theology of Liberation*
Edward Said's *Orientalism*
Gayatri Chakravorty Spivak's *Can the Subaltern Speak?*

PSYCHOLOGY

Gordon Allport's *The Nature of Prejudice*
Alan Baddeley & Graham Hitch's *Aggression: A Social Learning Analysis*
Albert Bandura's *Aggression: A Social Learning Analysis*
Leon Festinger's *A Theory of Cognitive Dissonance*
Sigmund Freud's *The Interpretation of Dreams*
Betty Friedan's *The Feminine Mystique*
Michael R. Gottfredson & Travis Hirschi's *A General Theory of Crime*
Eric Hoffer's *The True Believer: Thoughts on the Nature of Mass Movements*
William James's *Principles of Psychology*
Elizabeth Loftus's *Eyewitness Testimony*
A. H. Maslow's *A Theory of Human Motivation*
Stanley Milgram's *Obedience to Authority*
Steven Pinker's *The Better Angels of Our Nature*
Oliver Sacks's *The Man Who Mistook His Wife For a Hat*
Richard Thaler & Cass Sunstein's *Nudge: Improving Decisions About Health, Wealth and Happiness*
Amos Tversky's *Judgment under Uncertainty: Heuristics and Biases*
Philip Zimbardo's *The Lucifer Effect*

SCIENCE

Rachel Carson's *Silent Spring*
William Cronon's *Nature's Metropolis: Chicago And The Great West*
Alfred W. Crosby's *The Columbian Exchange*
Charles Darwin's *On the Origin of Species*
Richard Dawkin's *The Selfish Gene*
Thomas Kuhn's *The Structure of Scientific Revolutions*
Geoffrey Parker's *Global Crisis: War, Climate Change and Catastrophe in the Seventeenth Century*
Mathis Wackernagel & William Rees's *Our Ecological Footprint*

SOCIOLOGY

Michelle Alexander's *The New Jim Crow: Mass Incarceration in the Age of Colorblindness*
Gordon Allport's *The Nature of Prejudice*
Albert Bandura's *Aggression: A Social Learning Analysis*
Hanna Batatu's *The Old Social Classes And The Revolutionary Movements Of Iraq*
Ha-Joon Chang's *Kicking Away the Ladder*
W. E. B. Du Bois's *The Souls of Black Folk*
Émile Durkheim's *On Suicide*
Frantz Fanon's *Black Skin, White Masks*
Frantz Fanon's *The Wretched of the Earth*
Eric Foner's *Reconstruction: America's Unfinished Revolution, 1863-1877*
Eugene Genovese's *Roll, Jordan, Roll: The World the Slaves Made*
Jack Goldstone's *Revolution and Rebellion in the Early Modern World*
Antonio Gramsci's *The Prison Notebooks*
Richard Herrnstein & Charles A Murray's *The Bell Curve: Intelligence and Class Structure in American Life*
Eric Hoffer's *The True Believer: Thoughts on the Nature of Mass Movements*
Jane Jacobs's *The Death and Life of Great American Cities*
Robert Lucas's *Why Doesn't Capital Flow from Rich to Poor Countries?*
Jay Macleod's *Ain't No Makin' It: Aspirations and Attainment in a Low Income Neighborhood*
Elaine May's *Homeward Bound: American Families in the Cold War Era*
Douglas McGregor's *The Human Side of Enterprise*
C. Wright Mills's *The Sociological Imagination*

Thomas Piketty's *Capital in the Twenty-First Century*
Robert D. Putman's *Bowling Alone*
David Riesman's *The Lonely Crowd: A Study of the Changing American Character*
Edward Said's *Orientalism*
Joan Wallach Scott's *Gender and the Politics of History*
Theda Skocpol's *States and Social Revolutions*
Max Weber's *The Protestant Ethic and the Spirit of Capitalism*

THEOLOGY

Augustine's *Confessions*
Benedict's *Rule of St Benedict*
Gustavo Gutiérrez's *A Theology of Liberation*
Carole Hillenbrand's *The Crusades: Islamic Perspectives*
David Hume's *Dialogues Concerning Natural Religion*
Immanuel Kant's *Religion within the Boundaries of Mere Reason*
Ernst Kantorowicz's *The King's Two Bodies: A Study in Medieval Political Theology*
Søren Kierkegaard's *The Sickness Unto Death*
C. S. Lewis's *The Abolition of Man*
Saba Mahmood's *The Politics of Piety: The Islamic Revival and the Feminist Subject*
Baruch Spinoza's *Ethics*
Keith Thomas's *Religion and the Decline of Magic*

COMING SOON

Chris Argyris's *The Individual and the Organisation*
Seyla Benhabib's *The Rights of Others*
Walter Benjamin's *The Work Of Art in the Age of Mechanical Reproduction*
John Berger's *Ways of Seeing*
Pierre Bourdieu's *Outline of a Theory of Practice*
Mary Douglas's *Purity and Danger*
Roland Dworkin's *Taking Rights Seriously*
James G. March's *Exploration and Exploitation in Organisational Learning*
Ikujiro Nonaka's *A Dynamic Theory of Organizational Knowledge Creation*
Griselda Pollock's *Vision and Difference*
Amartya Sen's *Inequality Re-Examined*
Susan Sontag's *On Photography*
Yasser Tabbaa's *The Transformation of Islamic Art*
Ludwig von Mises's *Theory of Money and Credit*

Macat Disciplines

Access the greatest ideas and thinkers across entire disciplines, including

Postcolonial Studies

Roland Barthes's *Mythologies*
Frantz Fanon's *Black Skin, White Masks*
Homi K. Bhabha's *The Location of Culture*
Gustavo Gutiérrez's *A Theology of Liberation*
Edward Said's *Orientalism*
Gayatri Chakravorty Spivak's *Can the Subaltern Speak?*

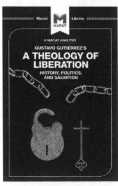

Macat analyses are available from all good bookshops and libraries.

Access hundreds of analyses through one, multimedia tool.

Join free for one month **library.macat.com**

Macat Disciplines

Access the greatest ideas and thinkers across entire disciplines, including

AFRICANA STUDIES

Chinua Achebe's *An Image of Africa: Racism in Conrad's Heart of Darkness*

W. E. B. Du Bois's *The Souls of Black Folk*

Zora Neale Hurston's *Characteristics of Negro Expression*

Martin Luther King Jr.'s *Why We Can't Wait*

Toni Morrison's *Playing in the Dark: Whiteness in the American Literary Imagination*

Macat analyses are available from all good bookshops and libraries.

Access hundreds of analyses through one, multimedia tool.
Join free for one month **library.macat.com**

Macat Disciplines

*Access the greatest ideas and thinkers
across entire disciplines, including*

FEMINISM, GENDER AND QUEER STUDIES

Simone De Beauvoir's
The Second Sex

Michel Foucault's
History of Sexuality

Betty Friedan's
The Feminine Mystique

Saba Mahmood's
*The Politics of Piety:
The Islamic Revival and
the Feminist Subject*

Joan Wallach Scott's
*Gender and the
Politics of History*

Mary Wollstonecraft's
*A Vindication of the
Rights of Woman*

Virginia Woolf's
A Room of One's Own

Judith Butler's
Gender Trouble

Macat analyses are available from all good bookshops and libraries.

Access hundreds of analyses through one, multimedia tool.

Join free for one month **library.macat.com**

Macat Disciplines

Access the greatest ideas and thinkers across entire disciplines, including

INEQUALITY

Ha-Joon Chang's, *Kicking Away the Ladder*

David Graeber's, *Debt: The First 5000 Years*

Robert E. Lucas's, *Why Doesn't Capital Flow from Rich To Poor Countries?*

Thomas Piketty's, *Capital in the Twenty-First Century*

Amartya Sen's, *Inequality Re-Examined*

Mahbub Ul Haq's, *Reflections on Human Development*

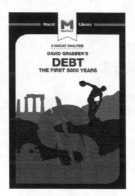

Macat analyses are available from all good bookshops and libraries.

Access hundreds of analyses through one, multimedia tool.

Join free for one month **library.macat.com**

Macat Disciplines

Access the greatest ideas and thinkers across entire disciplines, including

GLOBALIZATION

Arjun Appadurai's, *Modernity at Large: Cultural Dimensions of Globalisation*

James Ferguson's, *The Anti-Politics Machine*

Geert Hofstede's, *Culture's Consequences*

Amartya Sen's, *Development as Freedom*

Macat analyses are available from all good bookshops and libraries.

Access hundreds of analyses through one, multimedia tool.
Join free for one month **library.macat.com**

Printed in the United States
by Baker & Taylor Publisher Services